Oops, Pardon, Mrs Arden!

An Embarrassment of Domestic Catch Phrases

Nigel Rees

ROBSON BOOKS

This paperback edition first published in Great Britain in 2002
by Robson Books, 64 Brewery Road, London N7 9NT

A member of **Chrysalis** Books plc

British Library Cataloguing in Publication Data
A catalogue record for this title is available from the British
Library.

ISBN 1 86105 544 7

Typeset by FiSH Books, London WC1
Printed in Great Britain by Creative Print & Design (Wales),
Ebbw Vale

Oops, Pardon,
Mrs Arden!

Also by Nigel Rees and published by
Robson Books

As We Say in Our House

Introduction

This work has a predecessor – *As We Say In Our House: A Book of Family Sayings* (published in 1994) – dealing principally with those words and phrases that are unique to particular families. Often handed down the generations, this private language is sometimes unintelligible to outsiders, depending as it does upon the shared memory of some incident that gave rise to it. The family sayings had mostly been revealed to the outside world through my BBC Radio 4 programme *Quote... Unquote* and my appearances on Channel 4 TV's *Countdown*. It was apparent, however, that much of what people thought to be unique to their own families and circles was, in fact, part of a more widespread store of domestic catchphrases. So, the time has come to tackle this broader field of phraseology in a new book. *Oops, Pardon, Mrs Arden!: An Embarrassment of Domestic Catchphrases* is a compendium of sayings that have caught on, mostly in the home but also in informal situations. It does not concern itself with catchphrases whose origins lie in show business or advertising, except where these have a direct bearing on home and family matters.

As in the earlier book, I am immensely grateful to the thousands of listeners and viewers who have shared their domestic sayings with me. Often they tendered their offerings with some such remark as, 'Does anybody else say this?' Accordingly, in discussing the individual phrases, I have reflected the various homes and geographical areas in which I believe that usage has occurred. Attempting to date when a saying first entered the language and when it was notably current is an imprecise matter, but I have had a bash. Several of the entries that occurred in *As We Say In Our House* have benefited from notification of further usage by readers of that earlier book, as well as from additional information about origins and meanings. *Oops, Pardon, Mrs Arden!* is also enriched, I would hope, by the substantial feedback I have received when talking about family sayings and domestic catchphrases to several score Federations of Women's Institutes and Townswomen's Guilds, in England and Wales. Readers of *The "Quote...Unquote" Newsletter*, a subscription quarterly, have provided another invaluable source of supporting information.

Anyone who toils, as I do, in this area of popular speech, owes much to the late Eric Partridge, for having opened it up to (reasonably) academic scrutiny. I have always had a guarded appreciation of Partridge's rather questionable methods and conclusions, reserving my admiration for the reviser of his *Slang* and *Catch Phrases* dictionaries, Paul Beale. After Paul died in November 1999, I wrote in *The Times* of how he had 'a happy ability to recall colloquial usage from conversations and jokes during his career in the Army' and how the Partridge dictionaries 'benefited immensely from Beale's major revisions.' When it became plain that Paul would not be allowed to continue the task of revision indefinitely, he treated me to a stream of comments and suggestions, particularly on the catchphrase front. He also entrusted me with the material he had accumulated from many sources towards a further revision of the *Dictionary of Catch Phrases* after 1985. This has been duly incorporated in this book.

It will be obvious what a debt I owe to the thousands of enthusiasts who have written to me over the years with their recollections of domestic catchphrases. In particular, two contributors, Stella Richardson of Grays, Essex, and Rosaline Gibson of Sevenoaks, Kent, gave me substantial lists. In 1996, Mrs Gibson entrusted me with a notebook in which she had put down several score sayings used by her mother, Florence May Wickenden (1910–73). She commented: 'Coming from Kent farming people going back over 100 years...I wanted to write up some scenes from our life for my two daughters. We lived on the farm, Dad was a waggoner, plowman, then cowman. Mum had to work in the fields doing hard jobs like "thistle dodging". Some of the sayings could be termed vulgar.' But how excellent to have compiled this small memorial to remember her by. The phrases she used are simply indicated by the abbreviation (Wickenden).

There are several other sources to which I also refer, frequently, using these abbreviations:

Apperson:	G.L. Apperson, *English Proverbs and Proverbial Phrases* (1929)
Casson/Grenfell	Sir Hugh Casson & Joyce Grenfell, *Nanny Says*, ed. Diana, Lady Avebury (1972)
CODP:	*The Concise Oxford Dictionary of Proverbs* (1982)
ODP:	*The Oxford Dictionary of Proverbs* (3rd edn) (1970)
OED2:	*The Oxford English Dictionary* (2nd edn) (1989), (CD-ROM version) (1992)

Partridge/*Catch Phrases* Eric Partridge, *A Dictionary of Catch Phrases* (2nd edn, ed. Paul Beale) (1985)

Partridge/*Slang* Eric Partridge, *A Dictionary of Slang and Unconventional English* (8th edn, ed. Paul Beale) (1984)

As someone who entered this field from the more formal world of quotations, I have retained my natural instinct for attempting to establish the origins of these catchphrases. In some cases, it has been possible to establish their origins without doubt. But, as in all areas of folklore, it is a fairly forlorn expectation that this can be generally accomplished. On the whole, one just accepts that these phrases have 'caught on' because they appeal to something in the speaker, because they are fun, because they are easy-to-use, off-the-peg phrases, and because they are a simple way of dealing with life's little crises and embarrassments. In short, they are simply a means to get you through the day.

I should add that I have interpreted the word 'catchphrase' fairly broadly in writing this book. In fact, I have extended it to include various types of saying that I judge to have 'caught on' in the domestic environment. So, for example, I have included a number of proverbs or, at least, proverbial expressions, that are not strictly speaking catchphrases but which, nevertheless, are so much repeated that they have become honorary catchphrases.

In the entries, I have labelled some of the more common, specific types of catchphrase, thus:

fobbing-off phrases: a substantial sector this, of phrases used most often by parents to deal with the endless questions posed by their children: 'Why?' ('Y's a crooked letter');

'What's for dinner?' ('Bread and pullet').

initial code: a coded way of passing on advisory messages: 'T.T.T.', 'F.H.B.'

loophemisms: this describes the largest number of catchphrases in the book, having to do with euphemisms for going to the lavatory: 'I'm just going to turn the vicar's bike round'. The word 'loophemism' was coined by Frank Deakin of Wilmslow in 1995.

mangled words: a domestic trait common to many families is the deliberate mispronunciation of words, following accidental coinages: 'semi-skilled milk'; 'Nealopitan ice-cream'.

nannyisms: usually of a cautionary nature, these sayings may have been handed down by actual nannies or by grown-ups of a nannyish tendency: 'Back in the knife-box, Miss Sharp'.

proverbs: sayings that embody some general truth. Where I have been unsure that the saying has wide circulation and it does not have the force of a full-blown proverb, I have labelled it 'informal': as, for example, 'Custard boiled is custard spoiled.' This also applies to the type of instant observation that sounds like a proverb but may only have been coined by the speaker on the spur of the moment.

Wellerisms: a form of comparison in which a saying or proverbial expression is attributed to an amusingly inapposite source. Mieder & Kingsbury in their *Dictionary of Wellerisms* (1994) note that a Wellerism usually consists of three parts: a statement, a speaker who makes this remark, and a phrase or clause that places the utterance in a new light or an incompatible setting. The type was known long before Dickens gave a fondness for uttering these jocular remarks to Sam Weller. For example, from *The*

Pickwick Papers, Chap. 23 (1837): 'It's over, and can't be helped, and that's one consolation, as they always say in Turkey, ven they cut the wrong man's head off.'

Where a date is given after an informant's name, this refers to the year in which I received the information, not to when the phrase may have come into use.

Again, my thanks to everyone who has contributed to this little treasury and thus helped preserve these otherwise evanescent phrases.

Nigel Rees
Notting Hill, London

A

Africa. See GO AND LOOK AT...

age. See WE DO NOT NECESSARILY...

age before beauty... A phrase used (like 'after you...') when inviting another person to go through a door before you. The saying presumably originated when people first started worrying about the etiquette of going through doorways. It does not occur in Jonathan Swift's *Polite Conversation* (1738), as one might have expected it to do. It usually precipitated a response: 'If someone said to Mum, "Age before beauty", she would say: "S—t before the shovel, you mean"' (Wickenden). In the famous story, Clare Boothe Luce said 'Age before beauty' to Dorothy Parker, ushering her ahead. Parker assented, saying, 'Pearls before swine.' (Mrs Luce described this account as completely apocryphal in answer to a question from John Keats, Parker's biographer, quoted in *You Might as Well Live*, 1970.) A variant of 'age before beauty' reported from New Zealand (1987) is 'dirt before the broom', though Partridge/*Catch Phrases* has this as the *response* to that phrase (which it describes as a 'mock courtesy'). Yet other versions of the response are 'dust before the broom' (recorded in Dublin, 1948) and 'the dog follows its master'.

An exchange between two boozy buffoons at a pub door in Posy Simmonds's cartoon strip in the *Guardian* (19 May 1985) included the following: 'Certainly! Dogs follow their master!' 'Dirt before the broom!' 'Shepherd before sheep!' 'Shit before shovel!'

aired. See NEVER LIKES TO GET UP...

alive. See IF IT HAD BEEN ALIVE...

(I'm) all behind like the cow's tail. What people, like my wife, say when they are behind with their tasks. 'C.H. Rolph' wrote in *London Particulars* (1980): 'Grandma Hewitt [his grandmother] was a walking repository, rather than a dictionary, of clichés and catchphrases; and I have often wished she could have been known to Mr Eric Partridge during the compilation of his delectable dictionaries. Both she and I...could pre-date many of [his] attributions. Here are four examples...all of which were common currency in my Edwardian childhood: "Just what the doctor ordered", "Are you kidding?", "Cheats never prosper", and "All behind like a cow's tail".' There is also, of course, the expression 'All behind like Barney's bull'. Compare I'M LIKE BARNEY'S BULL...

all curtains and kippers. 'For a fine, well-appointed house but frugal "table"' – Harold E. Stock, Staffordshire (1999). Compare PLUS FOURS AND NO BREAKFAST.

all fur coat and no knickers. Describing a certain type of woman, given to show but having no modesty. Encountered by me in a Welsh context (1988), it was also the title of a play that toured the UK in the same year. A variant (1993), said to come from Lancashire (or, at least, from the North), is: 'Red hat, no knickers'. 'Fur coats and no drawers' was quoted by Stella Richardson, Essex (1998). A similar expression is 'all kid gloves and no drawers'. This last was given as an example of colourful cockney bubble-pricking by Kenneth Williams in *Just Williams* (1985). He said it was used in his youth (1930s) to denote the meretricious. Valerie Grosvenor Myer, Cambridgeshire, commented (1997): '"Silk stockings and no knickers" is another version, i.e. poverty concealed in an effort to keep up appearances.' Valerie sent a copy of *The Cambridge Insider* (2 October 1997) with its gloss that 'all fur coat and no knickers' means someone who appears elegant on the outside but is sleazy underneath.

all gong and no dinner. All talk and no action. What you would say of a loud-mouthed person, somewhat short on achievement. Current by the mid-20th century. On BBC Radio *Quote...Unquote* (20 July 1985), Anne Diamond, the TV presenter, said she had heard it in her father's family. Partridge/*Slang* has a citation from *The Archers* in 1981. Michael Grosvenor Myer, Cambridgeshire (1999), produced a Texan variant: 'All hat and no cattle.'

all good things must come to an end. On the completion of absolutely any activity that is enjoyable (but usually said with a touch of piety). *CODP* points out that the addition of the word 'good' to this proverb is a recent development. 'To all things must be an end' can be traced back to the 15th century.

all hat and no cattle. See ALL GONG...

all joints on the table shall/will be carved. Table manners instruction, i.e. elbows off. The actress Helen Lederer quoted this on BBC Radio *Quote...Unquote* (5 December 1989). Casson/Grenfell has this, as well as, 'No uncooked joints on the table, please'.

all kid gloves and no drawers. See ALL FUR COAT...

all mouth and trousers. Describing a type of man who is 'all talk', but possibly implying that he is also particularly interested in sexual matters (compare the earlier 'all prick and breeches'). Since the mid-20th century?

all over the place like a mad woman's underclothes. In her book *Daddy, We Hardly Knew You* (1989), Germaine Greer, the feminist writer, recalls that, when she was growing up in Australia, her mother's phrase – describing, say, an untidy room – was that it was 'all over the place like a mad woman's underclothes'. In consequence, Germaine used *The Mad Woman's Underclothes* as the title of a book of her assorted writings.

Partridge/*Slang* does not find this precise expression but, in discussing the phrase 'all over the place like a mad woman's shit', points to the euphemistic variants cited by G.A. Wilkes in *A Dictionary of Australian Colloquialisms* (1978): '...like a mad woman's knitting...custard...lunch box.' So, Australian it very much seems to be.

all prick and breeches. See ALL MOUTH...

all skin and grief. When seeing a thin or abnormally slim person: 'He's all skin and grief' – John Ellwood, Kent (1995).

all steps and stairs. A lump of bread cut awkwardly:

'That's all steps and stairs' (Wickenden).

all the shouting in the world won't make it right. 'When a person rails at cruel fate' (Wickenden).

alone. See GO WHERE KINGS...

always pull the strings on a banana – they give you stomach ache. A superstitious piece of nonsense that I certainly remember from my own youth (mid-20th century). Quoted in *More Momilies: As My Mother Used to Say*, ed. Michele Slung (1986).

...and the rest. 'My mother would never tell me how old she was. When I asked her she would answer, "Twenty – and the rest." She never would say how many years the "rest" was' – Andrew G. Forsyth, Hertfordshire (1996).

angel. See LIKE AN ANGEL WITH...

angels moving their beds. Thunder, as explained comfortingly to a child. 'The uncle and aunt who raised me in the 1920s taught me about thunder: "Don't be afraid – it's only the angels moving their beds"' – Ken Marshall, Basingstoke. Casson/Grenfell has the nannyism: 'Thunder is clouds knocking together'.

Annie. See UP IN ANNIE'S ROOM...

(put) another dog on the bed. What you do when it is cold. I first encountered this expression in an overheard remark collected by Cherry Lavell of London NW1 and broadcast on BBC Radio *Quote...Unquote* (28 November 1989): 'She said, "It's going to be very cold tonight, so I've put another dog on your bed, dear".' I have heard this saying repeated elsewhere but I am not sure whether it has really caught on.

answer. See 'NO ANSWER' WAS THE STERN . . .

(the) answer's a lemon. Fobbing-off phrase. 'My Cumbrian grandmother when asked a question would reply, "The answer's a lemon". "Why?" we asked – "Suck it and see," was her response' – Janet C. Egan, Middlesex (2000). This exchange brings together two well-known expressions, much used separately. 'The answer is a lemon', being a non-answer to a question or a refusal to do something requested of one, is probably of American origin and seems to have been in use by 1910. A lemon is acidic and sour, and there are several other American phrases in which a lemon denotes that something is unsatisfactory or not working properly. The lemon is also the least valuable object on a fruit machine. 'Suck it and see', meaning 'try out', presumably derives from what you would say about a sweet – 'suck it and see whether you like the taste of it'. It was used as a catchphrase by Charlie Naughton of the Crazy Gang, though it is probably of earlier music-hall origin – at least according to W. Buchanan-Taylor, *One More Shake* (1944). Partridge/*Slang* dates it from the 1890s. A correspondent, H.E. Johnson, suggested (1999) that it started with a *Punch* cartoon at the turn of the 19th/20th century, with the caption: 'First urchin: "I don't know if this here's a plum or a beetle." Second urchin: "Suck it and see".'

(to) answer the call of nature. Loophemism. Known since 1761, when Laurence Sterne, *Tristram Shandy* had that someone 'hearkened to the call of nature.' 'The calls of nature are permitted and Clerical Staff may use the garden below the second gate' – *Tailor & Cutter* (1852). 'Call of nature "sent [Robert] Maxwell overboard"...He would frequently get up in the middle of the night and found it more convenient, as a lot of men do on a boat, to relieve themselves over the side as it was moving' – headline and text, The *Independent* (21 October 1995). I have also encountered the variant, '(to) answer a certain requirement of nature'. The 'call of the great outdoors' may also be used in the same way. Originally the phrase 'great outdoors' was used simply to describe 'great open space' (by 1932).

any more for the Skylark? The age-old cry of swarthy fisher-folk inviting seaside visitors to take a trip around the bay, but now domesticated, as Partridge/*Catch Phrases* puts it, into a 'generalised invitation'. But how did it get into the language in the first place? A pamphlet (undated) entitled 'Any More for the Skylark? The Story of Bournemouth's Pleasure Boats' by L. Chalk tells of a whole series of 'Skylark' vessels run by a certain Jake Bolson at that seaside resort from 1914 to 1947. There is, however, a much earlier source. A researcher at the Brighton Fishing Museum revealed that a boat owner/skipper of those parts called Captain Fred Collins had owned many 'Skylarks' in his career. As he died in 1912, Collins was clearly ahead of the Bournemouth boats. Indeed, the *Brighton Gazette* had mentioned a 'new pleasure yacht, "The Skylark"' arriving from the builders in May 1852. The *Gazette*'s earliest citation of the actual phrase 'Any more for the Skylark' occurs in the edition of 17 November 1928 (in an article concerning Joseph Pierce, who took over from Collins). This does not explain how the phrase caught on beyond Brighton (perhaps through a song or stage-show sketch?) The edition of 8 May 1948 placed it among other pleasure boat cries: 'Brighton's fishermen ... will take their boats down to the sea and the summer season chorus of "Any more for the Skylark," "Half-way to China," "Motor boat going" and "Lovely ride out" will start again.'

anything for a quiet life. The Jacobean playwright Thomas Heywood used this phrase in his play *Captives*, Act 3, Scene 3 (1624), but Thomas Middleton had actually entitled a play *Anything For a Quiet Life* (possibly written with John Webster) in about 1620. Swift included the phrase in *Polite Conversation* (1738) and Dickens incorporated it as a Wellerism in *The Pickwick Papers*, Chap. 43 (1837): 'But anythin' for a quiet life, as the man said wen he took the sitivation at the lighthouse.'

apple. See WHAT'S WORSE THAN EATING ...

apples. See I'M CHUFFED ...

approbation from Sir Hubert Stanley is praise indeed. 'My parents were born in 1889 and 1895. One saying of theirs I remember very well indeed: "Commendation from Sir Hubert Stanley." It was a sort of damning with faint praise, or grudging admiration for some deed done' – Mrs B.M. Tomlinson, Essex (1996). There is no actual Sir Hubert Stanley in *Who Was Who* or the *Dictionary of National Biography*. However, there is a Sir *Herbert* Stanley, colonial administrator (1872–1955), who might fit the bill. But no, the origin of this remark is the line 'Approbation from Sir Hubert Stanley is praise indeed' which comes from the play *A Cure For the Heartache*, Act 5, Scene 2 (1797) by the English playwright Thomas Morton (?1764–1838).
Charles Dickens has 'Praise from Sir Hubert Stanley' in

Dombey and Son, Chap. 1 (1846–8). P.G. Wodehouse uses the expression as 'this is praise from Sir Hubert Stanley' in both *Psmith, Journalist*, Chap. 15 (1915) and *Piccadilly Jim*, Chap. 18 (1918). It is alluded to in Dorothy L. Sayers, *Gaudy Night*, Chap. 15 (1935): 'At the end of the first few pages [Lord Peter Wimsey] looked up to remark: "I'll say one thing for the writing of detective fiction: you know how to put your story together; how to arrange the evidence." "Thank you," said Harriet drily; "praise from Sir Hubert is praise indeed".'

arise, ye starvelings, from your slumber! 'When it was my father's job to wake up his two daughters in the morning, he would come in, draw the bedroom curtains and sing (he had no voice to speak of, so it was more like saying): "Arise, ye starvelings from your slumber!" – the first line of the Internationale. With this he was most familiar as an old time libertarian anarchist' – Oonagh Lahr, London N10 (1998).

arms. See THROWING HIS MONEY ABOUT . . .

arse. See I COULDN'T FANCY . . . ; IT SHONE LIKE A . . . ; NEITHER ARSE . . . ; TIGHT AS A DUCK'S ARSE . . . ; WANTS TO KNOW THE INS AND OUTS . . .

as awkward as a pig with side pockets. 'This is one of my mother's sayings which I have never heard anyone else use. She would say, "He/she is as awkward as a pig with side-pockets"' – Miss F.M. Smith, Hertfordshire (1995). Apperson finds 'as much need of it as a toad of a side pocket, said of a person who desires anything for which he has no real occasion', by 1785, and 'as much use as a cow has for side pockets', in *Cheshire Proverbs* (1917).

as black as Newgate knocker. H.E. Johnson, West Sussex, wrote (1994): 'My late mother often used an expression which must have had very old origins. If anything was very dark or dirty – all too frequently referring to myself or my attire – she would refer to it as being, "As black as Newgate's knocker".'

Indeed, this was once quite a popular comparison, known by 1881, and alluding to Newgate gaol, which was the notorious prison for the City of London until 1880. It must have had a very formidable and notable knocker because not only do we have this expression but, also, a 'Newgate knocker' was the name given to a lock of hair twisted to look like a knocker.

as He makes them, so He matches them. Said of any rather odd-looking married couple. Doris Humphrey, Lincolnshire, wrote (1995): 'I had an aunt who had an apt and witty saying for every eventuality – sometimes rather sharp and not very kind, but always apt' – and this was one of them.

(looked) as if they'd been learning Hebrew. Of wrinkled and untidy clothes – an expression used by the mother of Mrs Jean Wiggett, Kent (1995).

(you're) as lazy as Ludlum's dog who lay down to bark. 'My mother used to say this when one was reluctant to do the shopping or washing up...' – Joan Hartley, West Yorkshire (1998). Partridge/*Slang* has 'lazy as Ludlum's/ (David) Laurence's/Lumley's dog... meaning extremely lazy... According to the [old] proverb, this admirable creature leant against a wall to bark' and compares the 19th century 'lazy as Joe the marine who laid down his musket to fart' and 'lazy as the tinker who laid his budget to fart'.

Apperson has 'lazy as *Ludlam's* dog, that leant his head against a wall to bark' from Ray's proverb collection (1670).

as long as you've got your health, that's the main thing. A conversational cliché, together with its corollary, 'If you haven't got your health, you haven't got anything.' Current by the 1980s, at least.

as much use as a chocolate kettle. Phil Read, Staffordshire (1986) added to our stock of colourful expressions with this overheard remark at a Port Vale football match. It was made after the team had let slip another opportunity to score.

as much use as half a scissor. Said about a useless person – reported by Reg Stainton, North Yorkshire (2000).

as near as 'damn' is to swearing. Meaning 'too close to call', or 'no difference'. I first heard it from an optician at Liverpool in 1963.

as queer as Dick's hatband. Tony Brisby, Staffordshire, recalled (1992): 'A sentence used by my grandmother was, "He's as queer as Dick's hatband – it went round twice and then didn't meet." I have absolutely no idea what she meant.' Marjorie M. Rawicz, Nottinghamshire, remembered (1993): 'As a young person in the Twenties, I remember my Mother (Derbyshire with Yorkshire roots) saying "You're as funny as Dick's hat band" when either my sister or I was being contrary and difficult. I heard no more of this expression until the late sixties when a Miss Emily White (from Cheshire) told me that her Mother finished the quote – "Funny as Dick's hatband – it went twice round and then would not tie".'

David Scott, Cumbria (1994), remembered his grand-mother saying in the 1930s, if things didn't work out: 'That's like Dick's hatband – it went round twice and still didn't fit!' Dorothy Hoyle, Lincolnshire, added that, in her family, it was always 'as black as Dick's hatband' when something was very dirty. Mrs J.M.H. Wright, West Yorkshire, countered with: 'The correct version – "as *near* as Dick's hatband" – makes the saying self-explanatory, at least to a Yorkshire person. "Near" in Yorkshire speech as well as meaning "close to" also means "mean or stingy with money". Thus the person referred to is as "near" with money as Dick's hatband is "near" to Dick's head.' 'A botched-up job done with insufficient materials was "like Dick's hat-band that went half-way round and tucked"' – according to Flora Thompson, *Lark Rise*, Chap. 3 (1939).

So, lots of variations. The *OED2* gives the phrase thus: 'as queer (tight, odd, etc.) as Dick's (or Nick's) hatband', and adds: 'Dick or Nick was probably some local character or half-wit, whose droll sayings were repeated.' Partridge/*Slang* describes it as 'an intensive tag of chameleonic sense and problematic origin' and dates the phrase from the mid-18th to the early 19th century, finding a Cheshire phrase, 'all my eye and Dick's hatband', and also a version that went, 'as queer as Dick's hatband, that went nine times round and wouldn't meet.' In Grose's *Dictionary of the Vulgar Tongue* (1796), Partridge found the definition: 'I am as queer as Dick's hatband; that is, out of spirits, or don't know what ails me.' A 'Newcastle form c. 1850' is the 'nine times round and wouldn't meet', just given.

But who was Dick, if anybody? *Brewer's Dictionary of Phrase & Fable* (1989) was confident that it knew the answer: Richard Cromwell (1626–1712), who succeeded Oliver, his father, as Lord Protector in 1658 and did not make a very good job of it. Hence, Brewer's *Dictionary* (1989) believed, 'Dick's hatband' was his 'crown', as in the following expressions: 'Dick's hatband was made of sand' ('his regal honours were a "rope of sand"'), as 'queer as Dick's hatband' ('few things have been more ridiculous than the exaltation and abdication of Oliver's son') and 'as tight as Dick's hatband' ('the crown was too tight for him to wear with safety').

Compare what Harry Richardson, Surrey, remembered his grandmother (1870–1956) used to say in answer to a child's curiosity: '"You are as queer as a Norwegian fiddle"... I saw the artefact many years later. It has two frets!'

as the monkey said... The singer/songwriter Dillie Keane, speaking in 1990, revealed that, 'if as a child, you said you couldn't wait for something,' her Irish father would always repeat: 'As the monkey said when the train ran over its tail, "It won't be long now".' This last phrase, according to Partridge/*Slang*, is but one of the 'as the monkey said' remarks, where there is always a simple pun at stake: e.g. '"They're off!" shrieked the monkey, as he slid down the razor blade.'

ashes. See NO GOOD POKING THE FIRE...

ashtrays. See GO AND EMPTY...

ask your father what he's doing, and tell him to stop it. A frequent injunction, apparently, from the mother of the poet Michael Rosen (as he recalled in 1994). This saying was probably extrapolated from two quotations. The first, 'Go directly, and see what she's doing, and tell her she mustn't!', is from the caption by an anonymous cartoonist (possibly George Du Maurier) to a cartoon entitled 'EXPERIENTIA DOCET' in *Punch*, Vol. 63 (16 November 1872). The cartoon shows a girl asking her nanny, 'Where's baby, Madge?' Madge replies, 'In the other room, I think, Emily.' And then Emily comes up with this pronouncement. The second is from A.P. Herbert's 'Let's Stop Somebody From Doing Something' (1930): 'Let's find out what everyone is doing, / And then stop everyone from doing it.'

asparagus veins. Mangled words. Mrs Olga Sweeney, Devon (1995), listed this one among those used in her family: 'leg-ends' for legends; 'joe-beacon' for Jacobean; 'copper knickers' for Copernicus; 'super flewus' for superfluous; 'asparagus veins' for varicose veins. 'And we all use the term "hyperdeemic nerdle" (as heard on *It'll Be Alright On the Night*).'

aspirate. See HASPERATE...

aunt. See BOB'S YOUR UNCLE...; GO AND SEE ONE'S...

awkward. See AS AWKWARD...

B

baby. See THIS WON'T BATHE...

back. See I'LL SHOW YOU...; I'M SO HUNGRY...

back in the knife-box, little Miss Sharp. Nannyism. Addressed to a person with a sharp tongue. Compare 'you're so sharp you'll be cutting yourself'. Casson/ Grenfell also has: 'Very sharp we are today, we must have slept in the knife box/we must have slept on father's razor case/we must have been up to Sheffield'. Paul Beale found a homely example of the knife-box version in Donald Davie's autobiographical study *These the Companions* (1982): 'More than twenty-five years ago I [composed] a poem which has for epigraph what I remember my mother [in Barnsley, Yorkshire] saying when I was too cocky as a child: "Mr Sharp from Sheffield, straight out of the knife-box!"' Earlier than all this, Murdstone referred to David (in Chapter 2 of Charles Dickens, *David Copperfield*, 1849) as 'Mr Brooks of Sheffield', to indicate that he was 'sharp'. There was indeed a firm of cutlery makers called Brookes of Sheffield – a city which has for centuries been the centre of the English cutlery trade.

backside. See INS AND OUTS OF A . . .

bad cess to them! 'My Irish grandmother used to say this when she wished someone ill – a way of saying "Bad luck to them!" I only recently noticed it in Trollope's *The Macdermots of Ballycoran* (1847) – his first novel set in Ireland. The word "cess" refers to a tax or assessment levied in Ireland' – Elizabeth Seager, Oxfordshire (2000).

(a) bad cheese needs butter and a good cheese deserves it. Informal proverb – 'from my grandmother who died in 1955' – Joan Whitworth, Cumbria (1995).

baked. See I WOULDN'T FANCY . . .

banana. See ALWAYS PULL . . .

banjo. See GO FOR A QUICK . . .

Bardney. See DO YOU COME FROM . . .

bare-arsed. See YOU COULD RIDE BARE-ARSED . . .

barmy. See GINGER, YOU'RE . . .

barn. See SHINING LIKE SHIT ON . . .

Barney's bull. See ALL BEHIND LIKE . . . ; I'M LIKE . . .

bathe. See THIS WON'T BATHE THE BABY . . .

beans. See HOW MANY BEANS . . .

beautiful. See YOU MUST SUFFER . . .

bed. See ANOTHER DOG ON...; DRY BED...; HE CAN LEAVE...; PLEASANT DREAMS...; SOMEBODY GOT OUT OF BED...; WHAT A NAME TO GO TO BED...; YOU HAVE MADE...

bedclothes. See HANDS ABOVE...

Bedfordshire. See UP THE WOODEN HILL/STAIRS...

beds. See ANGELS MOVING...

beggars. See IF WISHES WERE...

behind. See ALL BEHIND...

Belgium. See REMEMBER BELGIUM!

believe. See I BELIEVE YOU...

belly. See BETTER THAN...; HOW'S YOUR BELLY...

benefit. See YOU WON'T FEEL THE BENEFIT...

(the) best doctors in the world are Doctor Diet, Doctor Quiet and Doctor Merryman. This nannyish sentiment goes back to Jonathan Swift, who included it among the clichés of *Polite Conversation* (1738). Nay, even further: Apperson has a citation from 1558 and the idea may be found in a poem by Lydgate (1449).

Theatre people have a similar expression that reflects rather the curative powers of getting on with the job – 'Doctor Greasepaint/Doctor Theatre will cure me.' Both versions were quoted in obituaries for the actress Irene Handl in November 1987 as being favourite phrases of hers. They not only suggest that acting is a cure for ailments, but also imply that actors *have* to be well most of the time to perform their function. The actor Bernard Bresslaw told me in 1991 that his preference was for 'Doctor Footlights will cure me'.

The creation of an imaginary doctor's name can also be found in the nickname 'Dr Brighton' for the healthy seaside resort.

better. See THIS, AND BETTER, MIGHT DO...

(I've seen) better legs on tables. A damning comment on a physical characteristic – Stella Richardson, Essex (1998).

better out than in. What you say when belching. Quoted in Mary Killen, *Best Behaviour* (1990). Or when farting, according to Partridge/*Catch Phrases*, where Paul Beale dates it to the 1950s.

(well, it's) better than a slap in your belly with a wet fish. Nannyism. 'I have a friend in her eighties whose Nanny always used to say this to her little charges, whenever one or other was complaining about something' – Anon, Surrey (1998). Partridge/*Slang* has 'slap in the belly' and Partridge/*Catch Phrases* has 'slap across the kisser'. The art critic Brian Sewell revealed on BBC Radio *Quote... Unquote* (12 April 1994) that his nurse, when bathing him, would not only inquire 'Have you done down there?', but also command him to stand up at the conclusion of the proceedings and whack him with a sopping wet flannel, saying, 'There's a slap in the belly with a wet fish.'

big. See YOU'RE BIG ENOUGH...

bike. See GO AND TURN...

Bill. See IT'S DARK / BLACK...

(a) bird never flew on one wing. 'My father would say this, whenever politely declining a second drink' – Hazel E. Simmons, London N20 (1998).

bitch. See EVERY DOG HAS...

bitten. See IF IT HAD BEEN ALIVE...

black. See AS BLACK...; IT'S DARK / BLACK...

blackout. See GO AND CHECK THE...

bleats. See EVERY TIME...

bless his little cotton socks! A pleasant remark to make about a child. As 'bless your little cotton socks', it just means 'thank you'. Partridge / *Slang* dates it from the turn of the 19th/20th century and labels it heavily 'middle-class'.

blessing. See IT'D BE A...

blind. See I SEE...; LUCK IS OUT WHEN...

(a) blind man on a galloping horse could see that. 'If I complained about something being not quite right, my late mother would say, "A blind man on a galloping horse would be glad to see that". I found myself saying it to the dentist when he fixed a crown and he thought it was hilarious' – Andrea Lowe, London NW10 (1996). Compare former Beatle Paul McCartney on the similarity between the sound of the Fab Four and the much later group Oasis:

'You would have to be a blind man on a galloping horse not to see it' – quoted by the Press Association (5 September 1996).

Wickenden has the simpler 'a blind man would like to see it', as said when you cannot sew a straight seam or line. '"Ah to be sure (condensed to 'Asher'), a blind man would be glad to see it," was frequently used by my Irish grandmother when I over-reacted to bumps, grazes or other minor blemishes. She would give the same rejoinder to the highlighting or criticism of any small imperfections in workmanship' – Brian Adams, Berkshire (1997). 'Rather than slave longer over some chore that was well enough done to pass, my mother would say, "A blind man would be glad to see it"' – Alison Adcock, Oxfordshire (1998).

Swift has 'a blind man would be glad to see that' in *Polite Conversation* (1738) and Apperson finds 'A blind man on a galloping horse would be glad to see it' by 1894. Compare the Australianism 'even blind Freddie could see that', for what is blindingly obvious, a phrase since the 1930s.

block. See I AM SPEAKING TO...

blood. See HELL'S BELLS...

blue. See ENOUGH BLUE...

blue-arsed. See RUNNING IN AND OUT...

boat. See COME OVER ON...

Bob's your uncle! 'And there you are/there you have it!/all will be well / it's as simple as that' – an almost meaningless expression of the type that takes hold from time to time. It was current by the 1880s but doesn't appear to be of any hard and fast origin. Basically a British expression – and somewhat baffling to Americans. There is the story of one such who went into a London shop, had it said to him, and exclaimed, 'But how did you know? – I *do* have an Uncle Bob!'

In 1886, Arthur Balfour was appointed Chief Secretary for Ireland by his uncle, Robert Arthur Talbot Gascoyne-Cecil, 3rd Marquis of Salisbury, the Prime Minister. Is that where the phrase came from, as some people fervently believe?

Miss M.L. King, London SW3 (1993), wrote: 'Whenever anyone says it, I reply, "And Fanny's your aunt" – I don't know why.' Peter Davies, Hertfordshire (1999), had rather: 'Bob's your uncle, Fanny's your aunt, and the baby's name is dripping.'

body. See KEEP BODY AND SOUL...

(go and) boil your head! I.e. 'go away, don't be silly!' Probably by 1900, especially in Scots use.

bone. See GOT A BONE...

Boney will get you. A curiously enduring threat. Although Napoleon died in 1821 (and all possibility of invasion had evaporated long before that), the threat was still being made in the early 20th century. In 1985, the actor Sir Anthony Quayle recalled it from his youth, and in 1990, John Julius Norwich remembered the husband of his nanny (from Grantham, interestingly) saying it to him in the 1930s. He added: 'And a Mexican friend of mine told me that when she was a little girl her nanny or mother or whoever it was used to say, "*Il Drake* will get you" – and that was Sir Francis Drake!'

boots. See GO AND SPLASH...; HE CAN LEAVE...; TROUSERS HAVE HAD A ROW...

born. See I WASN'T BORN...; JUST IN TIME...

Borneo. See WILD WOMAN OF BORNEO.

(well, she certainly fell with her) bottom in the butter. The writer Mark Steyn's mother is Belgian and, so he said (1989), is 'not very good at proverbs in English but uses a lot of Belgian expressions.' This is what she said 'when my third cousin eight times removed got married.'

bottoms. See HERE'S TO THE LORD...

bowels. See TRUST IN THE LORD...

boy. See MILES'S BOY TOLD...

brains. See FISH IS GOOD...

brass. See SAME TO YOU WITH BRASS...

bread and pullet [or **pullit**]. Fobbing-off phrase, when asked, usually by a small person, 'What's for tea?' – according to the writer Christopher Matthew on BBC Radio *Quote...Unquote* (16 May 1995). 'My Victorian grandmother also used the phrase "Bread and pull it". As she explained, you put a slice of bread into your mouth and pull it' – Robin Steers, East Sussex (1995). 'I was reminded of my grandmother's stock response. In childhood, I heard it as, "Bread and bread tillet", and took it as some kind of spread. Now I realise that she said "till it" (to it) being of Scots descent' – Margaret Mitchell, Merseyside (1995). 'When as a small child I asked my mother what was for dinner, I got "bread and pullit" or "What do you fancy, a parrot or a monkey?" or "Legs of chairs and pump handles"' – Enid Grattan-Guinness, Hertfordshire (1995).

'As many may think it has nothing to do with chicken (pullet), I believe it refers to the days when families were very large and there was not much money to feed them. The idea was that they would have a piece of bread and pull it as far as it would go, to make a small amount of food feed several people' – Sheila J. Wilberforce, Argyll and Bute (1996). 'My mother used to say "Bread and Pullett", supposedly a reference to a poor family who had to take the bread and pull it to make it go round' – Sylvia Dowling, Lancashire (1998). 'I recently came across a Victorian recipe for "Pulled Bread". The white crumb was peeled from the middle of a freshly baked, still warm loaf. This was then put in the oven until golden brown' – John Smart, Essex (2000).

breakfast. See PLUS FOURS AND NO...; SING BEFORE YOUR...; STOP PICKING YOUR NOSE...

breath. See SAVE YOUR BREATH TO...

breeze. See GOD BREEZE ME...

brick. See COUPLE OF...; GIVE SOMEONE THE...

brown. See WHEN IT'S BROWN IT'S DONE...

buckets. See HELL'S BELLS...

bug. See SNUG AS A BUG...

buggered. See WHEN IT'S BROWN IT'S DONE...

bull's foot. See DOESN'T KNOW PUSSY...

bum. See MY BUM IS NUMB...

bun. See PENNY BUN COSTS...

burn. See I DON'T MIND IF YOU...

burst. See GO FOR A QUICK...

(to) burst one's foo foo string. 'If any of us children were making exceptional physical efforts, my granny would say: "Be careful or you'll burst your foo foo string" – Dr Anthony Abrahams, Oxfordshire (1995). Partridge/*Slang* has the terms 'foo-foo band/powder/valve', also 'fu-fu' (a dish of barley and treacle), in none of which does the 'foo-foo' or 'fu-fu' have any discernible meaning. The fact that *foo-foo* is some sort of Chinese word for 'excrement' hardly helps us here...

bus. See FEEL LIKE A BUS...; SHUT YOUR MOUTH...

buses. See NEVER CHASE GIRLS...

bust. See HERE'S TO THE LORD...

butcher. See I AM SPEAKING TO...

butter. See BAD CHEESE . . . ; BOTTOM IN THE . . . ; FINE WORDS . . .

butter will be cheap when grass grows there. 'What you say when someone is scratching their back-side' – E.W. Wright, Suffolk (1995).

buttered. See FRIED FRAMLINGS . . .

buy. See NEVER BUY A SADDLE . . .

C

cabbage-looking. See NOT SO GREEN AS ...

call of nature. See ANSWER THE CALL ...

camel. See TRUST IN THE LORD AND TIE ...

can I press you to a jelly? 'I had an uncle who used to amuse my little friends at tea parties by saying he was so hungry he could "eat the dates off a calendar." He called my mother's fancy cakes "ooja-ka-pivs" for want of a special name and would say such things as "Can I press you to a jelly?" which made the small guests collapse in mirth' – Helen Rudge, Hampshire (1994).

(you) can lead a horse to water but... Informal proverb. 'My father, being a great one for the "bon mot" and the mixed metaphor, would say: "You can lead a horse to water but a pencil must be lead"' – Mrs Mary Froom, Devon (1995).

(he) can't help his looks but... 'My mother, speaking of someone she didn't like, would say, "I know he can't help his looks, but he could stop in"' – Mrs Margaret Wilson,

Cumbria (1996). Compare the story told by Abraham Lincoln: 'I feel like I once did when I met a woman riding on horseback in the wood. As I stopped to let her pass, she also stopped and looked at me intently, and said, "I do believe you are the ugliest man I ever saw." Said I, "Madam, you are probably right, but I can't help it." "No," said she, "you can't help it, but you might stay at home"' – quoted in *Abraham Lincoln by Some Men Who Knew Him*, ed. Paul M. Angle (1950).

carpet slippers. See HAVE ITS...

carved. See ALL JOINTS...

cat. See LIKE BILLY GIBBONS'...; LIKE THE BARBER'S...; SEE HOW THE CAT JUMPS...; THERE ARE MORE WAYS OF...; WHO'S SHE – THE CAT'S AUNT?

(has the) cat got your tongue? A challenge to the mute. The *OED2*'s earliest citation is H.H. Harper, *Bob Chadwick* (1911): 'I was so angry at her that I...made no answer...Presently she said, "Has the cat got your tongue?"' Perhaps usually addressed to small persons, and thus mostly a nannyism, as in Casson/Grenfell.

cats. See RAIN CATS AND DOGS.

cess. See BAD CESS...

(he has none of his) chairs at home. Elizabeth Monkhouse recalled (1997) that in her bit of Cheshire, 'He's got all his chairs at home' was an expression used to mean, 'He's all there, alert.' Hence, a home without furniture is empty, so 'no chairs at home' = empty headed, no longer at home, no longer 'there'. This was also reported from Lancashire. Meanwhile, Joyce Hanley wrote: 'In Yorkshire, if someone is a bit lacking in the head, we say that they haven't got all their furniture at home.' This information came to me when I was looking at the origin of the phrase 'to lose one's marbles', meaning 'to lose one's faculties', and was wondering whether it could have anything to do with the French word *meubles* (furniture). Apperson finds the Lancashire use by 1865, but also has a curious anticipation of the phrase by a man who writes, 'How slender furniture I have at home', referring to his accoutrements of 'eloquence, grace and good success.'

Charlie. See HOLD MY HAND ...

chase. See NEVER CHASE GIRLS ...

Chatham. See CHEER UP FOR ...

(it would be) cheap at half the price. I.e. cheap, very reasonable. Not a totally sensible phrase, dating probably from the 19th century. Presumably what it means is that the purchase in question would still be cheap and a bargain if it was twice the price that was being asked. In his *Memoirs* (1991), Kingsley Amis comments on phrases like this that perform semantic somersaults and manage to convey meanings quite the reverse of their literal ones. He cites from a soldier: 'I'd rather sleep with her with no clothes on than you in your best suit.'

cheer up for Chatham, Sheerness is in sight. 'The job is nearly finished' – John Titford in an article from his column in *Family Tree Magazine* (December 1994). Possibly from the approach to the port of Chatham by naval vessels that have to pass Sheerness first. Casson/Grenfell has the nannyism: 'Cheer up for Chatham! Dover's in sight' (though Dover is not as near to Chatham as Sheerness and would only be passed if the ship had come via the English Channel). The phrase 'cheer up for Chatham, wooden legs are cheap' was the subject of a correspondence in *The Times* (7 November 1986) and may point to a non-nautical provenance. One suggestion was that it referred to 'the Chatham Cheat, an old naval charity, which supplied wooden legs free to sailors who had lost theirs in action, together with a wound pension.' Other versions recalled were '...Dover's in sight' (as above) and '...Sheernasty [= Sheerness] is in sight', which were understood to refer to the old Kent railway, the London, Chatham and Dover (which had a branch line to Sheerness). Sheerness, like Chatham, was for centuries a naval dockyard.

cheese. See BAD CHEESE...; GORMLESS AS A...

Chicago. See GO AND CHECK THE PRICE...

chicken. See CHOKE UP...; IT FITS LIKE...

chimney. See WON'T GO OUT OF SIGHT...

chimney stack. See GIVE SOMEONE THE...

chimney sweep. See NEVER WRESTLE WITH...

chocolate kettle. See AS MUCH USE AS...

choke up, chicken – if it's only a bucketful, it'll ease you. 'I was an asthmatic and my mother used to say to me during an attack when coughing and wheezing, "Choke up, chicken, if it's only a bucketful it'll ease you"' – T.W. Tincombe, Norfolk (1996). 'My mother's family is from the West Midlands and it is customary when someone coughs to say (like "Bless you!", when someone sneezes), "Choke up, chicken; your mother was a duck!"' – Anon (2000). Partridge/*Catch Phrases* has 'Cough it up: (even) if it's only a bucketful, it will ease you' from the early 20th century. Apperson has various 'choke up' phrases, from 1605 onwards. Swift's *Polite Conversation* (1738) has: 'Choke, chicken; there's more a-hatching.'

chop. See NEVER SAY DIE...

chuffed. See I'M CHUFFED...

church. See THAT'LL STOP YOU FARTING...

Clarence. See HE WON'T BE CALLED...

clock. See FACE WOULD STOP...; GO AND SEE THE...

clogs. See GO AND SPLASH...; LIKE AN ANGEL WITH...

coast. See GO AND SEE A FRIEND...

cocks. See HANDS OFF...

(the) cocks may crow but it's the hen that lays the egg. Informal proverb. Uttered by Margaret Thatcher, when British Prime Minister, at a private dinner party in 1987 – according to Robert Skidelsky in the *Sunday Times*, Books (9 April 1989). On a London News Radio phone-in (December 1994), I was told: 'The cock does all the crowing but the hen lays all the eggs.' 'My grandmother's all-embracing put down of males: "He's a clever old cock, but he can't lay eggs'" – Margaret Rawles, Suffolk (2000). Apperson finds the obvious original, 'The cock crows but the hen goes', in use by 1659.

coffin. See IT'S NOT THE COUGH...

coin. See GOLD COIN SPEAKS...

colander. See LIKE A FART IN A...

cold hands, warm heart. A forgiving little phrase for when having shaken hands and found the other person's to be cold. A proverb first recorded in 1903 (*CODP*).

(I didn't) come over on the last boat, you know. 'Response to someone who has doubted your wisdom' – Stella Richardson, Essex (1998). Partridge/*Catch Phrases* has 'I didn't *come up* with the last boat' as a Royal Navy phrase from the mid-1940s, but also 'I didn't come up in the last bucket' and 'I didn't just get off the boat, y'know' for similar situations.

comfort. See GO AND PARTAKE OF...

convinced. See MAN CONVINCED...

corn. See LIVE HORSE AND YOU'LL EAT...

cost. See HOW MUCH DOES IT...

cotton. See BLESS HIS LITTLE...; TIGHT COTTON ALWAYS BREAKS.

cough. See IT'S NOT THE COUGH...

cough it up – it might be a gold watch. Said to someone having a coughing fit (Wickenden). Partridge/*Catch Phrases* has '…could be a gold watch', from the early 20th century.

(you) could grow potatoes in there. Said to children with dirty ears (Wickenden).

could I polish my skates? Loophemism. 'A Scotsman asking, "Where is the bathroom?"' – Mrs R.M. Robotham, Cambridgeshire (2000).

(you) couldn't knock the skin off a rice pudding. 'Said to a weak person or to a big-headed person' – Stella Richardson, Essex (1998). Partridge/*Catch Phrases* dates it from the First World War.

(you) couldn't punch a hole in a wet *Echo*. Said to a weak person – in Liverpool – Stella Richardson, Essex (1998). The *Liverpool Echo* is one of the city's newspapers. A local version of the more common 'couldn't punch your way out of a paper bag' which Partridge/*Catch Phrases* has as one of the variants of the previous phrase.

(a) couple of ha'pennies short of a shilling. Not very clever i.e. not the full twelve pence of a shilling (Wickenden). But one of a whole host of 'short of' phrases minted to describe mental shortcomings, or 'a deficiency in the marbles department' of someone who is 'not all there', and has either 'a screw loose' or 'a bit missing'. Other more venerable idioms for the same thing would include: that a person is 'eleven pence half-penny' 'not the full shilling'; 'tuppence short of a shilling'; 'only sixpence in the shilling'; 'ninepence to the shilling'. And some more on the 'short of' theme: 'a few vouchers short of a pop-up toaster' – I first noticed this one being used around May 1987; 'not quite enough coupons for the coffee percolator and matching set of cups'; 'one apple short of a full load'; 'one grape short of a bunch'; 'rowing with one oar in the water'; 'one card short of a full deck'; 'fifty cards in the pack'; 'not playing with a full deck'; 'one brick/a few bricks short of a (full) load'; 'a couple of bales shy of a full trailer load'; 'two sticks short of a bundle'; 'one pork pie/two sandwiches short of a picnic'; 'one can short of a six-pack'; and, 'two ants short of a picnic'.

(to) cover one's feet. Loophemism (archaic). 'And Saul went in to cover his feet' – 1 Samuel 24:3. David is hiding from Saul in a cave when in comes Saul to evacuate his bowels. Most modern versions of the Bible say, 'to relieve himself.' The Revised Authorised Version (1982) has: 'Saul went in to attend to his needs.' *The Living Bible* (Illinois, 1971) has, memorably: 'Saul went in to a cave to *go to the bathroom.*'

covering. See IT WILL BE A . . .

cow. See EVERYBODY TO THEIR . . . ; JOHNNY, GET YOUR GUN . . . ; LIKE A COW WITH . . . ; TUNE THE OLD COW DIED OF; WHY KEEP A COW . . .

cow's tail. See ALL BEHIND . . .

crafty as a wagon-load of monkeys. Very cunning (Wickenden). Compare the (apparently unconnected) cry to a group of people waiting to depart in a bus or coach: 'a cartload of monkeys and the wheel won't turn' – which Partridge/*Catch Phrases* suggests was current by 1890.

(a) creaking gate hangs longest. Of a (complaining) person in poor health who outlives an apparently healthier person. Apperson finds 'a creaking gate (or door) hangs long' by 1776. Other variants are: 'A creaking cart goes long on the wheels' (quoted as a common proverb in 1900) and 'creaking carts go a long way'.

cream. See THERE ARE MORE WAYS OF...

cripple. See EVERY CRIPPLE...

crow. See COCKS MAY CROW...

crows. See THAT'S JUST A FEW...

cry. See HAVE A GOOD CRY...

curtains. See ALL CURTAINS...

custard boiled is custard spoiled. Informal proverb. Told to me on a London News Radio phone-in (December 1994).

cut. See SLICE OFF A CUT LOAF...

D

daft. See YOU'RE AS DAFT...

daisies. See WHEN THE FIELDS ARE WHITE...

daisy. See GO AND PICK...

damn. See AS NEAR AS 'DAMN' IS TO...

dark. See IT'LL EITHER RAIN...; IT'S DARK/BLACK...; KEEP IT DARK...

dash my wig! Exclamation (archaic). The writer and jazz singer George Melly described on BBC Radio *Quote... Unquote* (27 May 1997), how his paternal grandmother exclaimed on being offered some (then rare) Danish Blue cheese in the late 1940s, 'Dash me wig, where did you get that?' This turned into a Melly family saying. When cheese was fancied, you said, 'I'll have a bit of dash-me-wig.' *OED2* has 'dash my wig' as a 'mild imprecation' by 1797. As 'dash my vig' the exclamation appears in R.S. Surtees, *Handley Cross*, Chap. 50 (1843). From *Punch* (20 February 1864): 'New Danish oath – "Dash my Schles-wig!"'

dead. See NEVER MIND, YOU'RE A LONG...

Dear Mother, it's a bugger! Sell the pig and buy me out.
'My father, a hard-working man, was always on the go,
muttering such things as, "Must soldier on,"or "Sell the
pig," or "Dear mother." He told me that when men
became soldiers they had to serve a minimum time and if
they wanted out sooner, they had to pay to leave the
army: hence the following correspondence from unhappy
son (in army), "Dear mother, sell the pig and buy me out."
And from mother to son, "Dear son, pig's dead. Soldier
on"' – Mrs Jay Carlyle, Edinburgh (1998). Partridge/*Catch
Phrases* dates this saying to about 1910.

despair. See WHAT SEEMS LIKE DESPAIR...

devil. See TELL THE TRUTH AND SHAME...

dew. See GO AND SHAKE THE...

diamonds. See I COULDN'T FANCY...

Dick. See AS QUEER AS DICK'S...

Dickie. See END UP IN...

Dicky. See STAY UP TILL...

(he) didn't come up on the down train. 'If my mother
thought someone was "street-wise", as we say today, she
would comment, "He didn't come up on the down train"'
– W.A. Vigs, Staffordshire (1996). 'My mother when being
teased would say, "Do you think I came up in a down
train?" and "I didn't come over with a foot in each funnel"'

– Keith Nixon, Biggin Hill (2000). The phrase 'up train' to describe a train going up to town (as opposed to the 'down train' coming down from town) was in use by 1841 and followed on from the earlier 'up coach' and 'down coach'.

die. See NEVER SAY DIE . . . ; WE'S ALL LIVE TILL WE DEE . . .

dies. See I HOPE YOUR RABBIT . . .

diet. See BEST DOCTORS . . .

(the only) difference between men and boys is the price of their toys. This modern proverbial expression has been credited both to Liberace and to Dr Joyce Brothers in the US. In the UK, there may be a difference: writer Derek Robinson talking in 1990 about the making of a TV version of his novel *Piece of Cake* said he noticed that everyone was fascinated by the Spitfire aircraft. All work would come to a stop whenever they were being used. A technician standing by remarked, 'You can tell the men from the boys by the size of their toys.'

dinner. See ALL GONG . . .

dirt. See AGE BEFORE BEAUTY; SO MEAN SHE WOULDN'T GIVE . . . ; WHAT SEEMS LIKE DESPAIR . . . ; YOU HAVE TO . . .

'Disappeario crescendo', as the monkey said when the marble clock fell over the precipice. 'I only ever heard my father say this. It could be said in consternation, when something suddenly fell; indignantly, if something suddenly went missing; quietly and resignedly, if something looked as though it had gone for good. And so on' – Mrs Frances George, Hampshire (1995). An incomprehensible Wellerism, indeed. Compare AS THE MONKEY SAID...

disaster. See NEVER DISCUSS A...

(you'd) disgrace a field of tinkers. Journalist John Walsh once described how his father, a West Coast Irishman, would say this of John's attempts to grow his hair long in the 1960s.

do. See IT DO, DON'T IT?

(to) do a two six. Mr E. Pettinger, Lanarkshire, inquired about a saying 'which was common among RAF ground staff when I was serving between 1945 and 1948. It was said when help was required in opening or closing the big hangar doors – "Two Six on the hangar doors!" I can still visualise the response following the shout. One had to stop what one was doing and help to push the enormous sliding doors.' Partridge/*Slang* dates it from 1930 and gives the definition, 'to do something very speedily and promptly'. Compare 'one-two, one-two', which a military person might bark with the same intention. Possibly from gun-drill – the number of a command in an instruction booklet?

Paul Beale commented (1993): 'Numbers Two and Six were part of the guncrew in Nelson's navy, or soon after, whose arduous task it was to heave the cannon back after firing so that Number something-else could swab it out, and yet another Number reload for (probably) Number One to light and fire again.'

(to) do by rock-of-eye and rule of thumb. 'My mother was trained to be a tailoress and in the work-rooms they always referred to things cut out without a pattern as "rock-of-eye". This word is also used in our family when cakes etc. are made without a recipe' – Betty Butcher, Wiltshire (1995). This is more widely known in the full expression (as in the headphrase). Partridge/*Slang* explains that it describes guessing instead of measuring precisely and suggests it originated in the tailoring trade in the mid-19th century. 'Rock' here means 'a movement to and fro'.

(to) do one's duty. Loophemism. Said by the father of Marjorie Wild, Devon (2000).

do you come from Bardney? Steve Race, the musician and broadcaster, wrote to me (1993): 'Small boys brought up in the city of Lincoln, as I was, will testify that if one left a door open, someone would be sure to say, "Do you come from Bardney?" Bardney is nine miles south-east of Lincoln and there was formerly an Abbey there, presumably with an "ever-open door".' Apperson finds this expression being discussed in *Notes & Queries* by 1905. Compare: 'Anyone who leaves a door open in Gloucestershire is liable to be asked: "Do you come from Winchcombe?" This is said to be a survival of the pilgrimage to Hayles, when the Abbot requested the good people of Winchcombe to throw open their doors to house the many pilgrims' – Eric R. Delderfield, *The Visitors' Brief Guide to the Cotswold Country* (1959).

doctors. See BEST DOCTORS . . .

(he) doesn't know pussy from a bull's foot. 'My father used to say this when referring to someone who didn't know what they were talking about. Is this (a) attributable and (b) rude?' – Richard Paul-Jones, East Sussex (1998). 'My (Bedfordshire) mother always used to repeat a saying of her own mother's to denote someone's ignorance – "He/she doesn't know A from a bull's foot". In recent years I said to her, "Surely it must have been *hay*, that would make more sense, but she insisted her mother had always pronounced it A' – Faith Moulin, Somerset (2000). Partridge/Slang has 'doesn't know a great A from a bull's foot' and 'does not know A from a battledore/windmill/the gable-end' (these last two versions known since 1401). There is also 'doesn't know B from a bull's foot' (1401), 'battledor' (1565) and 'broomstick' (undated). So we are definitely talking about the letter A rather than hay. I think all this means is that somebody cannot distinguish between the letter in a child's alphabet book and the object in question.

(he) doesn't know whether to shit or light a fire. 'My grandfather always says this of people who can't make up their minds. Apparently this refers to soldiers who, at the end of a long day's march can't decide whether to warm up first, or...' – Suzanne King, City of Glasgow (2000). Surprisingly, Partridge (with his army background) does not appear to know this expression. However, he does include (to describe ignorance rather than indecision): 'he doesn't know whether to shit or go blind/whether he wants a shit or a haircut/whether to scratch his watch or wind his ass', some of which are American in origin.

dog. See ANOTHER DOG ON...; AS LAZY...; EVERY DOG HAS...; GO AND SEE A MAN...; IN AND OUT LIKE A...; LET THE DOG SEE...; THERE'S LIFE IN THE OLD DOG...

dog bite old roper. 'In the 1920s, I worked with a man

who, learning of anything surprising, would say: "Well, dog bite old roper"' – L.A. Silver, Nottinghamshire (1994). This is rather a puzzle, except to note that 'roper' has been used as another word for 'hangman'.

(the) dog follows its master. See AGE BEFORE BEAUTY.

dogs. See RAIN CATS AND DOGS ; WE'S ALL LIVE TILL WE DEE...

doing. See ASK YOUR FATHER...

donkey. See LIKE A DONKEY EATS...; SO MISERABLE THAT...; YOU COULD ARGUE/TALK...

(I) don't feel like knocking doors out of windows. 'After 'flu, for instance, upon inquiry as to how I am feeling, I find myself saying, "Better, thank you, but I don't feel like knocking doors out of windows" – an expression from my Durham/Northumberland roots, perhaps?' – J. Allum, Suffolk (1998).

(he/she) don't go no further than Thursday. 'In Norfolk, of a person considered a bit simple, it was said: "He/she don't go no further than Thursday"' – Mrs Monica Nash, Nottinghamshire (1995).

don't make me laugh: I've got a cracked lip. Included by John Titford in an article from his column in *Family Tree Magazine* (December 1994). Partridge/*Catch Phrases* has '...I've got a split lip/I've cut my lip' and suggests that these extensions of the simple 'don't make me laugh' were moribund by the 1940s.

don't put your parts on with me. 'I was the thorn between two female roses in my pre-teens in the 1920s. Any misbehaviour, tantrums, etc. on the part of my sisters or myself, would be met by the rebuke from Mother: "Don't put your parts on with me!"' – Alan Beckerlegge, Lincolnshire (1996).

don't rush so, you'll be there before you start off. 'My own grandmother would say this to slow us down' – Mrs Stella Mummery, London SW14 (1995).

don't say 'No', if you'd rather not! 'A saying I recall is from an uncle who offered me the last slice of bread and butter, with the promise of a handsome husband, with £1,000 a year, if I ate it up. Then he'd say this' – Mrs M.M. Lockyer, London SE9 (1998). See also THOUSAND A YEAR.

don't some mothers have 'em? The comedian Jimmy Clitheroe (1916–73) was a person of restricted growth and with a high-pitched voice who played the part of a naughty schoolboy until the day he died. The BBC radio comedy programme *The Clitheroe Kid*, which ran from 1957 to 1972 popularised an old Lancashire – and possibly general North Country – saying, 'Don't some mothers have 'em?' In the form 'Some mothers do 'ave 'em', the phrase was used in the very first edition of ITV's *Coronation Street* (9 December 1960) and later as the title of a Michael Crawford series on BBC TV (1974–9).

don't stand there like one o'clock half struck; do something. 'My mother would say this when we (her five children) were mooning around' – Miss L. Williams, Greater Manchester (1993). Partridge/*Slang* defines 'like one o'clock half-struck' as 'hesitatingly' and finds it in use by 1876.

don't thank me, thank the Duchess. I don't know where this Duchess came from, but I was given the expression by Bob Hart, Powys (2000). There is a precedent for referring to some unnamed Duchess as a figure of benevolence or at least authority in the two sayings, 'ring up the Duchess!' and 'I must ring up the Duchess!' Partridge/*Catch Phrases* states that these sayings 'applicable to the resolution of a doubt or to the solution of a problem' caught on for a while following their use in the play *Young England* (1935).

don't you pour that tea, there will be ginger twins! 'My mother had some curious but firmly-held beliefs. The person who had made the tea, had to pour it. If it was poured by another it would bring ginger twins into the family. The reasoning behind this has baffled me all my life – though mother would hardly have welcomed twins of any colour, having already got a family of ten children' – Emily Howe, Suffolk (1994). There are, in fact, several superstitions concerning the pouring out of tea, especially if it involves two people. One is that it is bad luck for two people to pour out of a pot. Another (recounted in the journal *Folklore*, 1940) is this: 'I have often heard...that two women should not catch hold of a teapot at once or one of them will have ginger-headed twins within the year.'

don't you say things like that, you Toby, or I shall thump you with a big fat stick! Paul Beale wrote to me (1998): 'My diminutive grandmother used to threaten my uncle, 17 stone, and 6 feet tall, with this.'

door. See WHEN ONE DOOR CLOSES...

doors. See DON'T FEEL LIKE...

doorstep. See IT WILL TURN UP ON...

down. See DIDN'T COME UP...

drain. See GO AND DRAIN...

(to) drain one's snake. Loophemism. Attributed by Simon Raven to an army sergeant in one of his novels, in the form: 'He's gone to drain his snake.' Unconfirmed.

drawers. See ALL FUR COAT...

dreams. See PLEASANT DREAMS...

dressed. See FIRST UP...

drum. See PUT A PENNY ON THE...

Drury Lane. See LIKE A DRURY LANE...

dry. See MACKEREL SKY IS...

(a) dry bed deserves a boiled sweet. Nannyism (Casson/Grenfell).

dubs. See GO UP THE DUBS.

duchess. See DON'T THANK...; YOU CAN'T EXPECT...

duck. See TIGHT AS A DUCK'S ARSE...

ducks. See LOVELY WEATHER FOR . . . ; WHIMWAM FOR A GOOSE'S BRIDLE . . .

dust before the broom. See AGE BEFORE BEAUTY.

duty. See DO ONE'S DUTY.

E

E.B.B. (Eyes Bigger than Belly). Initial code, for a greedy person – reported by Janet M. Carr, Isle of Wight (1997).

E.C.M. (Early Christian Martyr). Initial code, 'for someone who feels themselves put upon' – told me by someone whose identity I have forgotten.

early. See YOU'VE BEEN ...

ears. See I WILL STICK ...; LITTLE PITCHERS HAVE ...

ease. See WE ARE NOT HERE FOR EASE AND SIN ...

eat. See YOU HAVE TO ...

eat well, work well, sleep well, and – well once a day. Informal proverb, probably seen as graffiti and quoted in Flora Thompson, *Lark Rise*, Chap. 1 (1939).

eels. See STEWED EELS AND ...

eke. See WE SHALL HAVE TO ...

elbow. See HAVING ELBOW...; NEITHER ARSE NOR...; UP AND DOWN LIKE A...

(an) elegant sufficiency. When declining an offer of more food, my father (1910–89) would often say, 'No, thank you, I have had an *excellent* sufficiency.' I have also heard people say, '...I have had an *ample* sufficiency' (as in the second episode of the TV *Forsyte Saga*, 1967), but neither of these is quite right. Paul Beale's *Concise Dictionary of Slang and Unconventional English* (1989) has the correct form, rather, as 'an elegant sufficiency...Jocular indication, mocking lower-middle-class gentility, that one has had enough to eat or drink, as "I've had an elegant sufficiency, ta!" since *c.* 1950.' In truth, 'elegant sufficiency' is the commonest of the three versions. Mary B. Maggs, Conwy, drew my attention (1998) to the fact that it is, after all, a quotation: 'My paternal grandmother, who died in 1956 aged almost ninety, would not, I think, have acquired anything that was possibly slang – she tended to model herself on Queen Mary and made a very creditable job of it. I remember it from the 1930s. Later I traced it to James Thomson, *The Seasons*, "Spring" (1746): "An elegant sufficiency, content,/Retirement, rural quiet, friendship, books".'

'I once heard two elderly ladies trying to piece together a much longer version of this, which went something like "I have had an elegant sufficiency of the appetising comestibles which you in your gracious hospitality so generously have provided", but I doubt if that is an accurate version as the only thing they could agree on was that it ended, "In other words – I'm full!"' – Sylvia Dowling, Lancashire (1998). Indeed, there would seem to be other jokey and verbose variations. 'From Wakefield in the 1890s, an aunt would say: "I've had quantum sufficio, an elegant sufficiency, and if I have any more I shall bust"'

– Miss D.F. Rayner, Surrey (1999). 'My mother would say: "I have had an elegant sufficiency. Any more would be an abundant superfluity"' – Lorna Cooper, Oxshott (1999).

'It has been suggested that "Ma'am, I've had elegant sufficiency. Any more would be an indulgence of my exasperated appetite" was what Lord Palmerston replied to Queen Victoria' – Deirdre Lewis, London W11 (2000). 'My mother used to say: "I have had an excellent sufficiency and any more would be superfluous to my palate"' – S.A.F., East Sussex (2000).

'My father (Jack Silver) when asked if he had enough to eat frequently replied, "Elephants and fishes eggs". When pressed, he explained it served for "an elegant sufficiency"' – Marion Ellis, Lincolnshire (1996). 'On the subject of strange family sayings, my late father would say after a meal either that he had had "an *ample* sufficiency" or "that's enough, no more, as it's not so sweet now as it was before"' – John Harrison, East Sussex (1995).

empty. See GO AND EMPTY...

end. See ALL GOOD...

(to) end up in Dickie's meadow. 'My grandmother used to say, "He'll end up in Dickie's meadow" to mean "in bad trouble"' – Mrs Monica van Miert, Tyne and Wear (1996). The allusion is to Bosworth Field, where King Richard III was famously defeated and killed in 1485. However, a simpler explanation has also been offered. Grose's *Dictionary of the Vulgar Tongue* (1811) defined 'dickie' as a 'donkey', so if you were in Dickie's meadow you were in the mire. See also AS QUEER AS DICK'S HATBAND.

(there's) enough blue to make a pair of sailor's trousers.

This saying is listed in Casson/Grenfell as an example of 'nanny philosophy': 'If there's enough blue sky to make a pair of sailor's trousers then you can go out.' *Brewer's Dictionary of Phrase and Fable* (1989) glosses it as 'two patches of blue appearing in a stormy sky giving the promise of better weather' and notes the alternative 'Dutchman's breeches' for 'sailor's trousers'. Indeed, 'Dutchman's breeches' would seem to be the original version, as stated in Smyth, *Sailor's Wordbook* (1867): '*Dutchman's breeches*, the patch of blue sky often seen when a gale is breaking, is said to be, however small, "enough to make a pair of breeches for a Dutchman".'

even if this was *good* **– I still wouldn't like it.** Richard Carrington, Gloucestershire (2000), wrote that he still employs this catch-all comment his father used when watching a TV programme or reading a book that didn't appeal to him. David Stead of South Tottenham then wrote to say that he had an old 78rpm record of a duo named Two Black Crows – Moran and Mack – on which one of them plays a few notes on a trumpet and the other says, 'Man, even if that was good – I wouldn't like it.'

evensong. See GO AND SEE THE VICAR...

every cripple has his own way of walking. 'A rather eccentric uncle lived with us for a while and if anyone queried his manner of doing anything, he always answered in this fashion' – Mrs Valentine Culmer, Hampshire (1996).

every dog has its day – and a bitch two afternoons! 'My mother, born in 1872, once told me that *her* mother, whenever a family member said something like, "Well,

every dog has his day," would mutter this response' –
Clare Meadmore, Cornwall (1994). Apperson finds the
addition to this proverb occurring by 1896 and – earlier, by
1864 – the 'Essex saying', 'Every dog has his day, and a cat
has two Sundays'. Patricia Nielsen, Aalborg, Denmark
(2000) had, from her Derbyshire father, 'Every dog has its
day and every cat its Saturday afternoon.'

**every little helps – as the old lady said when she piddled
into the sea.** Wellerism. 'My old Gran used to say it,'
remembered Jack O'Farrell, Cleveland (1994). In fact, lots
of people did/do. It is one of the best-known Wellerisms.
As, '"Every little helps," quoth the wren when she pissed
in the sea', it occurs in William Camden's *Remains
Concerning Britaine* (1605). The slightly politer, '"Every
little bit helps," said the lady, as she spit in the ocean', is in
John Dutton, *Letters from New England* (1867).

every time a sheep bleats it loses a nibble. Sometimes
rendered as 'Every time a sheep ba's it loses a bite'. H.L.
Mencken's *Dictionary of Quotations* (1942) has this as an
English proverb in the form 'Every time the sheep bleats it
loses a mouthful' and states that it was 'apparently
borrowed from the Italian and familiar since the
seventeenth century.' In this form it certainly appears in
Thomas Fuller's *Gnomologia* (1732). *CODP* finds a version
in 1599 and seems to prefer, 'A bleating sheep loses a bite',
explaining this as, 'opportunities are missed through too
much chatter.'

**everybody to their liking, as the old lady said when she
kissed the cow.** Wellerism. 'If family arrangements were
altered and she was told about it, my grandmother would
say: "Oh, well…anything for a change – as the old woman

said when she kissed her cow"' – Miss K.E. Bagley, Gloucestershire (1994). '"Chacun à son goût" said Kirsty (Christine) as she kissed the coo (cow)' – Tom Robertson, Tyne and Wear (1996). There are venerable early uses for this formula. Heywood's *Proverbs* (1546) has: 'Quoth the good man whan that he kyst his coowe.' Swift's *Polite Conversation* (1738) has: 'Why; every one as they like; as the good Woman said, when she kiss'd her Cow.' In Sir Walter Scott's *Peveril of the Peak*, Chap. 7 (1823), we find: '"She hath a right to follow her fancy," as the dame said who kissed her cow.'

everything a lady needs for sewing I have. 'I was a young schoolgirl soon after the First World War and lived near the Portobello Road in London. Most of the stallholders wore rough clothes and caps and mufflers – and had very Cockney cries, but one man wore collar and tie, a proper suit and bowler hat. He had a stall full of needles, pins, tape, elastic, press fasteners, and his cry, in a very high falutin' voice was: "Everything a lady needs for sewing I have". We youngsters (and our parents too!) took up this cry – and if *anyone* in my family and amongst our circle of friends ever asked anyone for anything, be it for sewing or not, we would hand the article over, and in our best rendition of the stallholder's voice, say, "Everything a lady needs for sewing I have!" Sadly, I now live alone, but to this day, if I can't immediately find something I want – a knife, pen, scissors etc., after hunting about and finding the article I will still say, in that same voice, "Everything a lady needs for sewing I have!"' – Miss F.M. Laughton, London N21 (1994).

everything comes to he who waits – only some of us wait a bloody sight longer than others. (Wickenden).

exaggerate. See HOW MANY HUNDRED...

expense. See HANG THE EXPENSE...

eye. See GOT YOUR EYE FULL?

F

F.H.B. (Family Hold Back). Initial code. Meaning that certain food in short supply is not to be eaten by members of the family when guests are present. Mentioned in Ian Hay's *Safety Match* (1911).

F.H.O. (Family Hold Off). Initial code.

F.K.O. (Family Keep Off). Initial code.

(to have a) face like a yard of pump-water. 'My mother would describe a person with a miserable expression as "having a face like a yard of pump water"' – Robert Stokes, Surrey (1997). Partridge/*Slang* has this as 'plain as a yard of pump-water', meaning 'very plain', by 1890. Apperson has 'straight as a yard o' pump water' (often said of a tall, lanky girl) as from Cheshire in 1886. Casson/Grenfell has, rather: 'Your *hair* is as straight as a yard of pump water.'

(that) face would stop a clock. Remembered by Stella Richardson, Essex (1998). Partridge/*Catch Phrases* gives a date of 1890 for this phrase and rather suggests that it would only be applied to a female.

fair. See HOW MUCH DOES IT...; IN AND OUT...

(the) fairies have been in. 'After a hard day at work I would sometimes come home to find Mum had done the housework for me. She would say: "The fairies have been in".' (Wickenden).

fairy. See LIKE A DRURY LANE...

family. See IT'S ALL IN THE FAMILY; RUNS IN THE FAMILY LIKE...

fancy. See I COULDN'T FANCY...; I WOULDN'T FANCY...

Fanny. See BOB'S YOUR UNCLE...

(the) far end of the fart. 'My mother, who was born in Lincolnshire, was wont to say of a person she considered too inquisitive: "He always wants to know the far end of the fart and where the stink goes"' – W.G. Wayman, Hertfordshire (1993).

Compare this from Anne Marie Hawkins, South Glamorgan (1994): 'My grandmother said of an inquisitive woman of her acquaintance: "She wanted to know the far end of a goose's trump, how many ounces it weighed, and which way the stink blew".'

fart. See FAR END OF THE... I'VE HEARD GEESE...; LIKE A FART IN A...

farting. See THAT'LL STOP YOU...

father. See IF YOUR FATHER HAD BEEN...

(to) feel like a bus on a wet day – full up inside. 'In

Newcastle-upon-Tyne, a lady we knew would say, "I feel like a bus on a wet day – full up inside"' – Mrs Monica Nash, Nottinghamshire (1995).

feet. See COVER ONE'S...

ferret. See LIKE A FERRET...

fiddle. See THERE'S MANY A TUNE...

fiddler. See UP AND DOWN LIKE A...

fields. See WHEN THE FIELDS ARE WHITE...

fight. See IF YOU CAN'T FIGHT...

fighting one minute and sucking each other's noses the next. On quarrelling kids: 'Don't interfere, they are...' (Wickenden).

find. See LOOK FOR ONE THING...

fine words butter no parsnips. This standard proverb, known since the 1630s at least, tends to get rattled off with little regard for its meaning or point, which is that 'fine words won't achieve anything on their own'. Or, as the other saying has it, 'Deeds not words'. Quite why parsnips are singled out is a puzzle, except that they are traditionally buttered up before serving. However, John Taylor, *Epigrammes* (1651) has this verse which shows that parsnips were not the only food mentioned in this regard:

> Words are but wind that do from men proceed,
> None but Chamelions on bare Air can feed:

Great men large hopeful promises may utter;
But words did never Fish or Parsnips butter.

Sometimes the word 'fine' is replaced with 'fair' (as in Casson/Grenfell) or 'soft'.

finger. See LET YOUR FINGER...

finished. See THEM AS FINISHED FIRST...

fire. See DOESN'T KNOW WHETHER...; NO GOOD POKING THE...; PLAY WITH FIRE...; GOT IT ALL ON...; YOU'D LAUGH TO SEE YOUR MOTHER'S...

first up...best dressed! 'My mother came from a large family and this was always her saying' – Mrs Smitten, Kent (1994). Partridge/*Catch Phrases* confidently asserts that this is an Australian phrase for circumstances 'where members of a family use each other's [or one another's] clothes.'

fish. See BETTER THAN...; WHAT'S THAT GOT TO DO WITH...

fish is good for brains. Nannyism. Casson/Grenfell has 'fish is good for the brain'.

fishing. See THIS IS NEITHER FISHING NOR...

fits. See IT FITS LIKE...

(it) fits where it touches. On loose clothing (Wickenden). Partridge/*Catch Phrases* has 'they fit where they touch' as applied originally to loose-fitting trousers (with a 1932 citation) and, since the 1960s, to suggestively tight clothes, especially trousers.

fix. See WHEN I SAYS 'FIX'...

fleas. See NIGHT-NIGHT SLEEP TIGHT...

fleet. See HEAVENS, ELEVEN...

fly. See RUNNING IN AND OUT...

foggy. See HAPPY DAYS...

foo foo string. See BURST ONE'S...

fool. See NEVER SHOW A FOOL...

foot. See I DON'T KNOW IF...; I'LL GO TO THE...; WANTS WAITING ON HAND AND...

(I've) forgotten more than you're ever likely to know.
Parent-child put-down. In her book *Daddy, We Hardly Knew You* (1989), Germaine Greer described how she had researched her father's history to find out the answers to questions about him that had always tantalised her. Along the way, she recorded Reg Greer's way of putting down children's questions. 'At the dinner-table where we children were forbidden to speak,' she wrote, 'he occasionally held forth...[but] if I pounced on some statement that seemed to me to reflect however dimly upon the real world [he would say], "I've forgotten more than you're ever likely to know".' Germaine commented: 'This fatuous hyperbole dismayed me...but perhaps after all it was literally true. Daddy's whole life was an exercise in forgetting.'

This would appear to be a venerable put-down. Something like it has been found in 1685. The proverb 'We

have all forgot more than we remember' was known by
1732.

fork. See LOOKED LIKE THEY HAD BEEN...; VINEGAR ON A FORK.

Friday. See TOMORROW WILL BE...

fried framlings and buttered haycocks. Fobbing-off
phrase. 'My Cumbrian grandmother when asked what
was for lunch would reply...' – Janet C. Egan, Middlesex
(2000). A haycock is a heap of hay in a field, but what a
framling is, I know not (except that Framling is the name
of a place in Hertfordshire).

friend. See GO AND SEE A FRIEND...; GO AND SHAKE
HANDS...; HELP YOURSELF...

Froochie. See GET AWAY TO...

full. See FEEL LIKE A BUS...

full of troubles nobody dies of. On being unnecessarily
miserable (Wickenden).

funeral. See YOU'D BE LATE...; TOO SLOW TO CARRY...

fur coat. See ALL FUR COAT...

furniture. See CHAIRS AT HOME...

G

galloping. See BLIND MAN ON...; WHY BOTHER?...

garden. See I'LL GO OUT INTO...; JOHNNY, GET YOUR GUN...; PARDON, MRS ARDEN...; UP/DOWN THE GARDEN PATH.

gate. See CREAKING GATE...

gaudy. See NEAT BUT NOT GAUDY...

geese. See I'VE HEARD...

Germans. See THAT'S ANOTHER MEAL...

get away to Froochie. 'What I have always imagined to be a family saying turns out to be a Scots expression. "(Go/get) away to Froochie," we used to say when I was a kid, meaning, "Stop talking nonsense/we don't believe you." There actually is a place called Freuchie in Fife, to which liars and leg-pullers could be sent. One of the Scottish papers not many years ago suggested it had some antiquity. My impression is that at one time Freuchie was well known, and had much the reputation in Scotland that Gotham had in England' – W.P. Brown, Aberdeen City (1994).

get off my leg, it's on a nettle. Included by John Titford in an article from his column in *Family Tree Magazine* (December 1994).

get your hat and knickers on. 'My father telling my mother to get ready to go out' – Doreen Casey, Buckinghamshire (1998).

Gibbons. See LIKE BILLY GIBBONS' CAT...

ginger. See DON'T YOU POUR...

Ginger, you're barmy! Addressed to any male, this street cry merely means he is stupid or crazy. It may date from the early 1900s and most probably originated in the British music-hall song with the title 'Ginger, You're Balmy [the alternative spelling]!' written by Fred Murray and published in 1912. This was sung by Harry Champion (1866–1942). In the song the next phrase is 'Get your hair cut!' Also, in the chorus, there occurs another line sometimes coupled with the 'Ginger, you're barmy!' – 'Why don't you join the army'. *Ginger, You're Barmy* was used as the title of a novel (1962) by David Lodge.

Separately, the word 'ginger' has been applied in the UK to male homosexuals (since the 1930s, at least) on account of the rhyming slang, 'ginger beer' = 'queer'. 'Ginger' is also the name given to a red-headed man. But neither of these appears relevant to the song. Ian Gillies commented (1995): 'The plot of "Ginger" is very similar [to another Champion song] "Any Old Iron" – someone who fancies himself well dressed, being shouted at in the one case because of his "old iron" watch-chain, and in the other because he isn't wearing a hat and not, apparently, because he is ginger. Indeed, there is no specific reference to his being ginger.' Here are the lines:

'Don't walk a-bout with your cady [= hat] on;
Ginger, you're balmy!
Get your hair cut!', they all be-gin to cry.
'With nothing on your nap-per, oh, you are a pie!

Pies must have a lit-tle bit of crust,
Why don't you join the army?
If you want to look a don you want a bit of something on –
Ginger, you're balmy!'

girls. See NEVER CHASE GIRLS...

(to) give someone the topmost brick off the chimney stack. 'When someone adored another person: "He'd give her the topmost brick off the chimney stack if she wanted it"' (Wickenden). Partridge/*Slang* suggests that the phrase 'to give someone the top brick off the chimney' means 'to be the acme of generosity, with implication that foolish spoiling, or detriment to the donor would result, as in "his parents'd give that boy the..." or "she's that soft-hearted, she'd give you..."' Partridge's reviser, Paul Beale, who inserted this entry, commented that he had heard the phrase in the early 1980s but that it was probably in use much earlier. Indeed, when Anthony Trollope was standing for Parliament in 1868, he described a seat at Westminster as 'the highest object of ambition to every educated Englishman' and 'the top brick of the chimney'. Casson/Grenfell includes, 'Very particular we are – it's top brick off the chimney or nothing.'

In 1985, Denis Thatcher, husband of the then Prime Minister Margaret Thatcher, was quoted as having said: 'I like everything my beloved wife likes. If she wants to buy the top brick of St Paul's, then I would buy it.' Presumably,

Denis was reworking the chimney stack version for his own ends. Unconsciously, he may also have been conflating it with another kind of reference, such as is found in Charles Dickens, *Martin Chuzzlewit*, Chap. 38 (1844): 'He would as soon have thought of the cross upon the top of St Paul's Cathedral taking note of what he did...as of Nadgett's being engaged in such an occupation.'

glazier. See IF YOUR FATHER HAD BEEN...

glutton. See MUSTARD ON MUTTON...

gnash. See THEM AS 'ADN'T TEETH...

(to) go and check the blackout. Loophemism. 'I'm just going to check the blackout' – Frank Deakin, Cheshire (1996).

(to) go and check the plumbing. Loophemism – volunteered by S. Davison, Nottinghamshire (1996). Also: '(to) go and inspect the plumbing' – Adrian D. Bull, North Yorkshire (1998).

(to) go and check the price of wheat in Chicago. Loophemism. 'My husband Peter, who is Canadian, goes "to check the price of wheat in Chicago"' – Edith Pink, Fife (1995). Dr Pink adds: 'The origin dates back to the 1920s when my husband Peter's grandfather had a seat on the Toronto Stock Exchange and had at one time almost cornered the market in wheat futures! Of course, all was lost in the crash of '29, but the saying persisted in the family.'

(to) go and drain one's radiator. Loophemism. 'I'm going to drain my radiator' – S. Davison, Nottinghamshire (1996).

(to) go and empty the ashtrays. Loophemism. 'We lived in a terraced house, with no inside toilet or hot water, and when my mother was going to make the beds, she armed herself with a bucket and said, "I'll just go and empty the ashtrays"' – I. Moore, Greater Manchester (1994).

(to) go and empty the teapot to make room for the next cup of tea. Loophemism. 'Another one is that I "am going to make room for a cup of tea"' – Hazel Stretton-Ballard, Buckinghamshire (1996).

go and lie in the graveyard until God calls you! 'When we children used to complain about feeling ill – wanting a day off school – my mother would say this' – Patsy Howson, Herefordshire (1995).

(to) go and look at Africa. Loophemism. 'My father used to say "I'm going to look at Africa", despite the fact that we were living in India!' – Mrs R. Collins, Norfolk (1998).

(to) go and lower the level. Loophemism. Adrian D. Bull, North Yorkshire (1998).

(to) go and partake of a minor [or major] comfort. Loophemism. 'My one time chief, Fleming-Williams, used to offer visitors a minor comfort or a major comfort' – Clement R. Woodward, Hertfordshire (1995).

(to) go and pick a daisy. Loophemism. Partridge/*Slang* has this as 'mostly women's' use by 1860 and notes that a 'daisy' was also the name for a chamber-pot, possibly because of the floral design on it.

(to) go and pump ship. Loophemism. 'My late father

always used to say he was going to "pump ship"' – Molly Anderson, Herefordshire (1996).

(to) go and wring out one's socks. Loophemism. 'My usual saying, "I've got to go and wring out my socks"' – Ted Farley, Kent (1996).

(to) go and see a friend off to the coast. Loophemism. Revealed by the actor Jon Glover on BBC Radio *Quote...Unquote* (30 May 1995).

(to) go and see a man about a dog. Loophemism. A caption to a Ghilchik cartoon in *Punch* (22 January 1930) is: 'The Age Old Excuse. Cave-dweller. "I won't be long, dear. I've just got to see a man about a brontosaurus".' A little strangely, Partridge/*Catch Phrases* seems to suggest that this phrase originally indicated that the man was about to 'visit a woman – sexually', then that he was 'going out for a drink', and then that he gave it 'in answer to an inconvenient question'. Only fourthly does it list 'go to the water-closet, usually to "the gents", merely to urinate.' At one time, *Brewer's Dictionary of Phrase and Fable* also preferred the 'concealing one's destination' purpose of this phrase, suggesting that it was a late 19th century American expression, and giving an example of its use during Prohibition as disguising the fact that the speaker was going to buy illegal alcohol from a boot-legger. A later edition suggested that the phrase meant that the speaker was pretending that he would see a man about placing a bet on a dog race.

I'll stick to what I take to be the primary meaning. It has been suggested that 'dog' is some sort of rhyming slang for 'bog', a well-known term for a lavatory, but this is not true rhyming slang and does not convince me.

(to) go and see if one's hat is on straight. Loophemism. 'I always say, "I am just going to see if my hat's on straight", not that I ever wear one' – Mrs Jean Koba, Berkshire (1996). 'Asking if one wanted the loo when leaving, Jim remarked that Lady Lloyd, wife of George (Lord) Lloyd, proconsular figure to whom Jim was formerly secretary, used to enquire: "Do you want to put your hat straight?"' – Anthony Powell, *Journals 1982–1986* (1995).

(to) go and see one's aunt. Loophemism. 'As I was the youngest of six children (and the only boy) I was often surprised by the affection shown to their relations by various friends of my elder sisters. "Just going to see my aunt" was an expression I must have heard hundreds of times in my youth' – R.W. Tincombe, Norfolk (1996). Also Trevor Ffoulkes (2000).

(to) go and see the man I joined up with. Loophemism. I.e. joined up in the army with – J. Skinner, Kent (1996).

(to) go and see the Turk – Mustapha Pee. Loophemism. Mrs Mac, Inverness-shire (1996).

(to) go and see the vicar and book a seat for evensong. Loophemism. 'An uncle of mine many years ago, when wanting to visit the loo, would say, "Shan't be long, just going to see the vicar and book a seat for evensong"' – Miss Nonnie P. Jaram, Isle of Wight (1998).

(to) go and see what time it is on the market clock. Loophemism. 'My mother always said: "I'm just going to see what time it is with the market clock"' – Frank J. Thomas, Bedfordshire (1995).

(to) go and shake hands with the wife's best friend.
Loophemism. D. Jones, Merseyside (1995). Partridge/
Catch Phrases also lists the variations: '...with my best
friend', '...with an old friend', '...with the unemployed'.
Also: 'I am just going to shake hands with the father of my
son.'

(to) go and shake the dew from one's orchid.
Loophemism. Told to me at a WI Federation meeting in
Cumbria-Westmorland (1997). Compare: '"Must shake the
dew off my violet" – said by my father' – Dave Hopkins,
Kent (1998).

(to) go and shed a tear for the widows and orphans.
Loophemism – adduced by Molly Anderson, Hereford-
shire (1996). 'My friend Floss always says, "I'm just going
to shed a tear"' – Ruby A. Richardson, Cleveland (1996).
Both these probably derive from the famous expression
'I'm going to shed a tear for Nelson'.

(to) go and sit on the throne and rain over my subjects.
Loophemism. 'My favourite expression is, "I am going to
sit on the throne and rain over my subjects".' Hazel
Stretton-Ballard, Buckinghamshire (1996).

(to) go and splash one's boots. Loophemism. Anon,
Somerset (1996). Also 'splash one's *shoes*'.

**(to) go and splash one's clogs as one's back teeth are all
awash.** Loophemism. John Hill, Dorset (1996).

(to) go and squeeze a peach. Loophemism. 'My late and
very dear friend James McLean was for eleven years
Private Secretary to HM Sultan Qaboos Bin Saeed, Sultan
of Oman. James always leaned forward and down to my

ear especially at cocktail parties and whispered, "Where can I go to squeeze a peach?"' – Allan Wilson, Merseyside (1996). 'A friend of mine, who is eight months pregnant, said as she headed for the loo: "I must go and squeeze a kidney!"' – Sonja Bailey, Kent (1995). Hardly a euphemism at all...

(to) go and stand up. Loophemism. The poet John Betjeman's term for urinating was 'standing up' (as opposed to 'sitting down', naturally). He would say: 'I must go and stand up' – *Letters*, ed. Candida Lycett Green, Vol. 1 (1994). 'As a very small boy I knew no other expressions than that I wanted "to stand up" (or "to sit down"), which seemed logically obvious and simple to me, but I can't remember what my sisters used to say' – Peter Newbolt, Norfolk (1997).

(to) go and telephone Hitler. Loophemism. 'In France in the war, members of the Resistance used to say "I'm going to telephone Hitler" ' – Mrs Nan Bourne, West Midlands (1997). I recall that my uncle, Group Captain Tom Gleave, a Battle of Britain pilot, used to say, 'I'm going to make a telephone call to Hitler.' Were he to be called away again, he would say, 'Here comes the reply...'

(to) go and turn one's bike round. Loophemism. Widely used, as in, 'I'm just going to turn my bike round.' 'I have heard that one being used here in Suffolk and was given this explanation. Back in the days when policemen used cycles on the beat, the Suffolk and Norfolk bobbies would meet on the county boundary. They had a chat, attended to the wants of nature, then "turned their bikes round", hence the old saying!' – Marie Laflin, Suffolk (1995). 'At a recent tennis tournament at our small village club one of our ladies (middle-aged like myself) left the court saying "I'm just going to turn the vicar's bike round"' – Mrs H. Ball, Buckinghamshire (1996).

(to) go and wash one's hands. Loophemism. 'Friends of ours had a Swiss student staying with them to improve his English and he had been told that the British always say "Would you like to wash your hands?" if inquiring whether a visitor wished to use the lavatory. So one day our friends brought him to afternoon tea with us and we first of all wandered around our large garden. On entering the house afterwards, I really thought Willy needed to wash his hands, but upon asking him, he replied, "Oh, no thank you. I have washed my hands behind a bush in your garden!"' – Anon, Cambridgeshire (1996).

And then there is: '(to) wash one's hands before the train gets into the station' – Mr O. Barry, West Sussex (1996).

(to) go and wash the car. Loophemism – reported by Margaret Walsh, Auckland, New Zealand (1987).

(to) go and water the horse(s). Loophemism. '"I'm just going to water the horse" (spoken with a strong Black Country accent)' – Frank Deakin, Cheshire (1996).

(to) go and water the lilies. Loophemism – reported by Margaret Walsh, Auckland, New Zealand (1987).

(to) go for a quick burst on the banjo. Loophemism. 'A former colleague and friend used to say: "I'm going for a quick burst on the banjo." He picked it up when doing his National Service in the RAF. Apparently, the colloquial Japanese word for latrine is "benjo"' – Douglas J. Bolger, Dorset (1995).

(to) go for a sweet one. Loophemism. 'I knew a refined lady who used to go for "a sweet one" (= a sweet pea)...' – Mrs D.M. Broom, Berkshire (1996).

(to) go for a wee walk. Loophemism. 'A friend with whom I used to ramble said, on wishing to disappear into the bushes, "I'm just going for a wee walk"' – Winifred Marks, West Midlands (1996).

(to) go North. Loophemism. 'When I was a Girl Guide many years ago we used to call it "going north". Can you imagine our amazement when one day the main headline in one of the national papers read: KING GOES NORTH – CROWDS FLOCK TO SEE HIM. It's absolutely true – I swear it!' – Norah Mayland, West Midlands (1996). It has been suggested that this usage may have been inspired by Noël Coward's song 'The Stately Homes of England' (1938): '...And the lavatory makes you fear the worst./It was used by Charles the First,/Quite informally,/And later by George the Fourth/On the journey North.' *Punch* (28 August 1886) had the headline 'Going North!', but over a piece on trains.

(to) go out without one's hat on. 'In our family, "He's gone out with his hat on" means that whoever you're speaking to, isn't listening (usually because they are reading the newspaper!)' – Betty Walker, Merseyside (1998). Partridge/ *Slang* has 'hat on = formally dressed', which may not be much help.

(to) go through. Loophemism. 'I trained as a nurse at Barts in the 1940s and the expression used by us was "going through". The saying originated because in years gone by the sisters lived on the wards and had their bedrooms at the far end, but no toilet facilities. When they wanted to go to the loo at night a bell was rung and the patients put the bed clothes over their faces as sister "went through"' – Mrs E.M. Richard (1996).

(to) go to do a job no one else can do for one. Loophemism. Partridge/*Catch Phrases* suggests this dates from about 1950.

(to) go to La Pomme. Loophemism. 'Many years ago when I was nursing, the term used was "La Pomme". I never discovered why' – Mrs B. Jenkins, Cardiff (1996). 'The toilet at the Royal Victoria Infirmary [Newcastle] was "the La-Pom"' – A.O. Harbron, Tyne and Wear (1996). Now how does this come about? I can only observe that, in French, *la pomme d'arrosoir* = the rose of a watering can, and that *c'est une pomme à l'eau* = he's/she's a real twerp, nerd. Also there is the fact that 'la' = lavatory/latrine in certain Australian usage.

(to) go to page 54. Loophemism. Joan Hassall (1906–88) was an artist and wood engraver. Betty Roe told me (1995) that this was Joan's polite way of referring to the matter. 'I'm going to page 54,' she would say.

(to) go to Paris. Loophemism. 'In my House at school it was traditional to say "I'm going to Paris" for the lavatory – which, not surprisingly, distressed the French under-matron' – Philippa Lawrence, Wiltshire (1996). Presumably, this derives from 'to go to P'?

(well, I'll) go to Putney on a pig! An expression of surprise or astonishment. Partridge/*Slang* has, however, that 'go to Putney (on a pig)!' was the equivalent of saying 'go to Hell!' In whichever way it was used, the lure of alliteration seems the predominant reason for the phrase.

(to) go to the off-stump. Loophemism. 'Among a group of my friends – all ex-Army National Service – we use the expression "going to the off-stump". This derives from a cricket commentary we once heard where the commentator said something like – "He's just had a slash over the off-stump"' – Rex Lanham, Hampshire (1996).

(to) go to the smallest room. Loophemism. The *OED2*'s earliest citation for this phrase also contains another loophemism: 'It is all very baffling for the uninitiated foreigner, who when his host offers to "show him the geography of the house" finds that his tour begins and ends with the smallest room' – A. Lyall, *It Isn't Done* (1930).

(to) go up the dubs. Loophemism. 'In the 'thirties I went to a small village school in Wales, and when we wished to visit the lavatories, we would say, "I'm going up the dubs." I've never heard that expression since I left that school but only recently did I realise that it must have been a shortened version of WCs' – Mrs Thelma Collyer, Kent (1996).

(to) go upstairs. Loophemism. Even in flats.

(to) go where kings go alone. 'I was working in an office and a female Latvian sat next to me. When a male member of staff had left the office and was wanted on the phone etc., our Latvian friend would say: "He has gone where Kings go alone". Similarly when a female was missing, she had always gone "where the Queen goes alone"' – Miss Rosemary C. Black, West Midlands (1995). The Revd John Hagreen, Kent (1996), added: 'I heard the euphemism "*Où* *le roi va seul"* in southern France in the late 1920s.' Prof. Robin Jacoby, Oxfordshire (1999), mentioned the Russian euphemisms: 'I'm going where even the Tsar goes on foot' and 'I'm going where even the Tsar removes his gloves.'

God. See GO AND LIE IN ...; MAN IS AS GOD MADE ...

God breeze me for a damned sausage. 'From my dad. I.e. "Well, I never" or "Damn and blast" – I *think*. So obscure, yet I never asked him for a translation but it is regrettably too late now! – Graham Davies, Lancashire (1996).

(she's) going through a phrase. Nannyism (Casson/ Grenfell). And well she might be if she is reading this book.

gold. See COUGH IT UP ...

(a) gold coin speaks in any language. Proverb. 'When travelling, Father always carried a few sovereigns and when asked why, the reply was: "A gold coin speaks in any language"' – Miss O.E. Burns, West Midlands (1995).

gong. See ALL GONG ...

good. See ALL GOOD ...; EVEN IF THIS WAS ...

good Gordon Highlanders! 'My father-in-law had a number of pet sayings, mainly from the First World War I think – like the expletive, "Good Gordon Highlanders!" Whenever life became a bit difficult he would say: "Everything's in favour against us!" Another, not actually used by him as a "saying" but which instantly became a part of the family's language, and still is: fuming over his cleaning lady's latest saga of breakages, he spat out: "She does not know it yet – but that lady is due for non-retention!" – which is now the standard description in our household for anything that has to be emptied out!' – P. Skilling, London W2 (1996).

(a) good woman will draw a man further than gunpowder would blow him. 'My father-in-law used to say this' – Violet Cowley, Buckinghamshire (1995). Compare: 'Crumpet can pull you further than gunpowder can blow you' – father's advice from a London News Radio phone-in (December 1994).

goose. See WHIMWAM FOR A GOOSE'S BRIDLE...

Gordon Highlanders. See GOOD GORDON...

(you're as) gormless as a ha'porth of cheese in a washing mug. 'Said by my mother' – Stella Richardson, Essex (1998).

(I've) got a bone in my leg. All-purpose excuse for non-activity. 'If you wanted to show mum something and said "Come here, mum," she would say: "I can't, I've got a bone in my leg"' – E.W. Wright, Suffolk (1995). This humorous excuse – sometimes '...in my throat/arm/etc.' goes back to the 16th century, as Apperson makes clear.

Anthony Fisher recalled (1997): 'As a child in the early forties I would frequently summon my father to come upstairs to read me a story. He obviously found this a rather tiresome chore and to relieve him of this duty my mother would reply, "He can't come now, he has a bone in his leg". Even at my early age, I thought this a pretty, er, lame excuse as mobility would have been even more difficult without a bone in his leg – but what on earth could have been the origin of this curious expression?' I think it is fairly pointless seeking a reason for this feeble excuse. The obviousness of the statement – like 'he's got two ears on his head' – is an indication that the excuse is not to be taken in any way seriously. Whatever the case, it is a venerable idiom. Jonathan Swift included it among the conversational clichés in his *Polite Conversation* (1738) – which shows it must have had whiskers on even then:

> *Neverout:* Miss, come be kind for once, and order me a dish of coffee.
> *Miss:* Pray, go yourself; let us wear out the oldest first. Besides, I can't go, for I have a bone in my leg.

(she's) got it all on in case of fire. 'My mother, on seeing someone rather over laden with jewellery, would comment...' – Hazel E. Simmons, London N20 (1998).

got your eye full? 'In Norfolk, if someone thought you were staring at them, they'd say: "Got yer eye full?" (which sounded like "got yer rifle?")' – Mrs Monica Nash, Nottinghamshire (1995).

grass. See BUTTER WILL BE CHEAP...; LIVE HORSE AND YOU'LL GET...

graveyard. See GO AND LIE IN...

gravy. See SAME THING, DIFFERENT...

green. See NOT SO GREEN AS...

grief. See ALL SKIN...

grow. See COULD GROW...

grumble. See IF YOU'VE GOT THE...

grunt. See WHAT DO YOU EXPECT FROM A PIG...

guess. See YOU COULD GUESS...

gun. See JOHNNY, GET YOUR GUN...

gunpowder. See GOOD WOMAN WILL...

H

half. See CHEAP AT HALF...; PUT A HALF ON TOP...

halfpennies. See COUPLE OF...

halfpenny. See YOU TALK LIKE...

hand. See HOLD MY HAND...; I'LL SHOW YOU...

hands. See COLD HANDS...

(all) hands above the bedclothes, girls! 'I overheard this said by one of three women in their late twenties who were in a tea-shop in Kensington on their way to an old girls' reunion. There were giggles galore as they all chorused in recollection' – Edward V. Marks, Surrey (1994). Compare:

hands off cocks, on with sock(s). As though delivered as a wake-up call to a men's dormitory (in the army, Boy Scouts, or wherever), I first encountered this cry in a play called *Is Your Doctor Really Necessary?* at the Theatre Royal, Stratford East in 1973. Partridge/*Catch Phrases* suggests an early 20th-century British Army origin and the slightly more elaborate form: 'Hands off your cocks and pull up your socks!'

hang the expense – throw the cat another kipper. 'My grandfather would say this if he or anyone else was contemplating a mild extravagance' – Jane Klemz, North Yorkshire (1994). 'I have always heard this as "hang the expense, throw the cat another goldfish" (the tie-up being the inclusion of expense and gold)' – Owen Friend, North Devon (1996). Compare TO HELL WITH POVERTY...

ha'porth. See GORMLESS AS A ...

happy as a skylight. 'We have a mother known for her gems. She always insisted that so long as my father had his pint, pipe and piano, he was: "happy as a skylight"' – Alison Rosenberg, London N10 (1995).

happy days and foggy nights! 'A family friend (ex-Royal Navy) used to say this to me when he said goodbye' – Diane Jeffrey, Suffolk (1999). 'Happy days' is presumably the traditional toast but 'foggy' may bear one of its other meanings, i.e. tipsy.

harder when there are none, my dear. Fobbing-off phrase. 'Here are a few my Mum used to say to us children all them years ago. When we complained, "Mum, these crusts are so hard", she would say "Harder when there are none, my dear"' – Mrs Tickner, Surrey (who was 84 in 1994).

hasperate your haitches, you hignorant hass, or I'll 'it you on the 'ead with an 'ard 'ammer and make you 'owl 'orrid. 'Whenever our accents slipped up as children my mother would say this...[it] must be said with the necessary refined emphasis on the "haitches" in the first half, followed by a real fishwife for the second!' – Jocelyne Newman, West Sussex (1998).

hat. See GET YOUR...; GO AND SEE IF...; GO OUT WITHOUT...; HERE'S YOUR HAT...; IF YOU CAN'T FIGHT...

hatband. See AS QUEER AS DICK'S...

have a good cry, get it out of your system. 'My mother used to say to me, when I was a child, bumped or scraped myself, and wanted to cry, "Be brave, don't cry". So I decided that I would love my little ones better whenever they needed it! And my comfort phrase became, "Have a good cry, get it out of your system." Until one day I was comforting my then 13-year old daughter after a nasty tumble, with my special phrase, and, between sobs, in puzzled tones, she asked: "*Why* do you *always* say, 'Have a good cry, get it out of your sister?''" – Lesley Prosser, Powys (1994).

(to) have a whistle. Loophemism. 'One of the many euphemisms for male urination – particularly among the boating fraternity' – John Phillips, Looe (*sic*), Cornwall (1996).

(to) have its carpet slippers on. 'My grandfather observing a silent fart: "That one had its carpet slippers on"' – Betty Roe, London W10 (1995). The writer Andrew Davies was quite open in referring to his mother-in-law's expression after a fart: 'Oh, it's just a little wee one in its stockinged feet' (on BBC Radio *Quote...Unquote*, 10 May 1994). Compare SILENT BUT DEADLY.

have you got a match?/I haven't got one to match you. (Wickenden).

haven't I been telling you for the past half hour, I'm coming in a minute? 'My mother used to say this' – E. Jean Crossland, Nottinghamshire (1994).

having elbow pie. 'My grandmother – early 1940s – if you had your elbows on the table, would say, "You don't want anything to eat – you're having elbow pie"' – William W. Bishop, London SE24 (1998).

hay. See IT'S THE SIGN OF...

haycocks. See FRIED FRAMLINGS...

he can leave his boots/shoes under my bed anytime. Meaning, 'I find him sexually attractive'. This was said to me by a small lady of Iranian extraction regarding Robert Redford (in April 1970). As far as I know, she's still keen.

he won't be called Clarence any more... 'Always quoted when a fly was killed or, later on, whenever anybody got killed in a radio or TV programme: "*He* won't be called Clarence any more..." I think it came from a melodrama my parents saw in their courting days in the very early 30s, possibly at the New Cross Empire' – Enid Grattan Guinness, Hertfordshire (1992).

Betty Burke, Wiltshire (1993), came up with a possible source. She remembered from her schooldays an example in an English grammar book ('probably illustrating the accusative case') – 'They used to call him Clarence, but they call him nowt now, for I murdered him last Monday.'

Poor Clarence, whichever one he was! He had an interesting death, of course, and not with a fly-swat, in Shakespeare's *Richard III*. Indeed, it was suggested (2000) that 'he won't be called Clarence any more' was an overheard playgoer's reaction to the murder of Clarence in *Richard III*.

Partridge/*Slang* remarks of the name: 'Like, though less than, *Cuthbert*, apt to be used as a jocular colloquialism.'

Paul Beale told me: 'A *Punch* cartoon of 2 February 1916 may be relevant; it shows an officer and a sergeant discussing a distant sentry: '*Officer.* "Why do you think he wouldn't make a good corporal?" *Sergeant* (*indicating sentry*). "'I'm a corporal! Lor Lumme! Why, 'is name's Clarence!'"

heads. See LOOK OVER YOUR HEADS...

health. See AS LONG AS YOU'VE...; IF YOU HAVEN'T GOT...

heaven help the sailors on a night like this! 'My grandmother on the North East coast would exclaim this when the wind howled around the house' – Ian Forsyth, Co. Durham (2000). Compare, from Partridge/*Catch Phrases*: 'Pity the poor sailor on a night like this!'; 'God help sailors on a night like this'; and 'God help the poor sailors...'

heavens, eleven o'clock and not a whore in the house dressed! When Derrick Carter, Suffolk, wrote to the radio show in 1991 to tell us about an unusual saying of his mother's, he cannot have foreseen the wave of nostalgia he was precipitating. Whenever her domestic programme was falling behind badly, Mr Carter remembered, his mother would say, regardless of the time: 'Heavens, eleven o'clock and not a whore in the house dressed!' But where had she got this expression from? Mr Carter remarked that both his parents were keen theatre-goers in the 1920s and 30s, and he wondered if his mother might have been quoting a line from a play – though whether one can imagine such a sentiment getting past the blue pencil of the Lord Chamberlain's Office in the days of stage censorship, is a different matter.

What is interesting about this expression is that, whereas

most 'family sayings' are incomprehensible to outsiders, this one was known to many more *Quote...Unquote* listeners. Mona Howard of Hampstead said she believed the full version was, rather: 'Heavens, eleven o'clock and not a whore in the house dressed, not a po emptied, and the streets full of Spanish sailors...' Jo Smithies, Isle of Wight, recalled the maternal: 'Heavens! four o'clock and not a whore washed and the street full of sailors.' Christopher J. Anderson, Surrey, came up with his mother's subtly different, 'Heavens! Ten o'clock! Not a bed made, not a po emptied, not a whore in the house dressed, and the Spanish soldiers in the courtyard!' Maude Gifford, Suffolk, said her mother used to say, 'Goodness gracious me, not a girl washed and the street full of Spanish soldiers!' Miss M.L. Fountain of Wembley passed on to us that her brother recalled it, not as a mother's saying, but as something he heard in his days in the Navy, in the form: 'Ten o'clock already – no pos emptied, no beds made and a street full of matelots.'

F.H. Loxley, Bristol, dated from 1944 his first hearing of the cry (in the *Army*): 'Eight o'clock, and not a whore in the house washed and a troopship in the bay.' Vernon Joyner, Surrey, on the other hand, settled for: 'Eleven o'clock, not a whore washed, not a bed made, and the *Japanese fleet* in town!'

Turning, as we do, to the works of Eric Partridge, we find that he only once gave his linguistic attention to the comparatively simple phrase 'eleven o'clock and no pos emptied' – though 'no potatoes peeled' and 'no babies scraped' are mentioned as variants. In Paul Beale's revision of Partridge/*Catch Phrases*, there is a 1984 reference to the version used by Terry Wogan on his breakfast radio show (after giving a time-check) – '[It's eight twenty-five]...and not a child in the house washed.'

Indeed, the saying has a pronounced Irish air to it. John Millington wrote (1998): 'My wife's mother was from Dublin and spoke of going to the Gate and Abbey theatres before the 1914–18 war. I have seen and heard plays by various Brendans, Seamuses etc. but have never come across this. It was, and still is, said when an unexpected, but known, visitor arrives: "The gas man! Come in, Sir, excuse the cut of the place, Sir. Not a child in the house washed yet, himself coming in any minute and no-one to go for the soap".'

The 'whores/pos/sailors' version is possibly a colourful elaboration of this basic expression. But how do so many people know it? Perhaps, after all, it might have escaped the stage censor's blue pencil. One could certainly imagine a pantomime dame attempting something similar. In the 1980s, the comedian Les Dawson is reliably reported to have uttered the 'no pos emptied' line in drag. Rupert Hart-Davis in *The Lyttelton Hart-Davis Letters* (Vol. 3, 1981) writes in a letter dated 9 June 1958: 'In the words of the harassed theatrical landlady, "Half-past four, and not a po emptied".' Whether all or part of the expression is a quotation from a play, or not, one does keep on being drawn back to a possible theatrical origin. The earliest printed reference found to date is in the *Spectator* (24 April 1959). Patrick Campbell recorded that 'Ten-thirty, and not a strumpet in the house painted!' was a favourite saying, apparently round about the late 1930s, of Robert Smyllie, editor of the *Irish Times*.

Ravey Sillars of the Isle of Arran told me (2000) that her father, who had fought in the First World War, and who died in 1940, used to say, 'Look at the time – and not a whore in the house *painted!*'

An even more substantial variant was reported to me by M. Stratford, Isle of Wight (1998): 'My mother, busy with five children, suddenly realising the time was getting late, would look at the clock and exclaim, "Good grief, six o'clock and no sausages pricked!"' Again, Jillian Oxenham, Pembrokeshire, wrote (1994): 'Although my Cornish husband categorically denies that his mother ever said this, in the seafaring communities of Cornwall, on inquiring, and being told, what time it was, a gasp was often followed by this memorable phrase: "Not a whore in the house washed and Jack coming up the road!"' E.N. Rouse, Worcestershire, wrote (2000): 'Father when asked the time would say: " — o'clock, and Lizzie not here yet." Could this be related in some way?'

Hebrew. See AS IF THEY'D BEEN...

heels. See SLIPPERY HEELS.

Hell's bells and buckets of blood. 'An expression of annoyance, remembered from the 1930s' – Mrs M.B. Bedwell, West Sussex (1996). Partridge/*Slang* has this as a 'mock ferocious' extension of the basic 'Hell's bells!' = hell!

help yourself – and your friends will like you. Bryan Magee, the philosopher and broadcaster, recalled on BBC Radio *Quote...Unquote* (26 April 1994) that when his grandfather was offered something with the words, 'Help yourself...', he would reply softly: 'And your friends will like you.' This I take to be based on the Scottish proverb, 'Help thyself, and God will help thee' which has been known since the 18th century. Casson/Grenfell has the nannyism: 'Help yourself and your friends will love you', but this is obviously derived from what we find in Swift's *Polite Conversation* (1738): 'Come, Colonel, help your self, and your Friends will love you the better.'

hen. See COCKS MAY CROW...; LICKS HEN RACING.

hens. See SHAKE YOURSELF AND GIVE...

Herbert. See TURN 'ERBERT'S FACE TO THE WALL.

here. See WHY ARE WE HERE?...

here's to the Lord in whom we trust – if it wasn't for our bottoms our bellies would bust. 'My mother would say this after a good meal' – Mrs H. Acklin (aged 82), Essex (1998).

here's your hat, what's your hurry? Bill Cotton, the TV producer and executive, recalled on BBC Radio *Quote...Unquote* (17 November 1998), that his mother would say this when a party went on too long. Also: 'I like your company, but your hours don't suit.'

Hesperus. See WRECK OF.

hind. See YOU COULD ARGUE/TALK...

hips. See MOMENT ON YOUR LIPS...

Hitler. See GO AND TELEPHONE...

hold my hand and call me Charlie. 'We say this to our children when crossing the road' – Gail Cromack, Carmarthenshire (1998). Partridge/*Slang* describes this as 'a mostly derisive catch phrase usually addressed by youth to girl: 1930s.'

holus-bolus. 'My father, a World War I soldier, used the expression "Olus Bolus" if a task was not very well done, or done slapdash' – Kathleen Lacey, Devon (1998). The *OED2* has an entry for this word and suggests a dialect origin, apparently a mock-latinisation of 'whole bolus' (where bolus is Latin for 'a good haul'), or of an assumed Greek word for 'whole lump'. The *OED2* defines the word as 'all at a gulp; all in a lump; all at once' and has a citation from 1847 to 1878. Quite how this became an expression for shabbiness is not clear. Compare however 'olo piecee' = anything shabby, in Partridge / *Slang*, described as pidgin for 'old piece' and dating from about 1905.

home. See JUST THINK IF WE LIVED...; LET'S GO SO THAT WE...; WHAT'S THAT WHEN IT'S AT...

Home, James, and don't spare the horses/This night has been ruined for me. 'A phrase often used for many years in my family' – Jane Williamson, Angus (1998). More usually just as, 'home, James, and don't spare the horses', this is a catchphrase used jocularly, as if talking to a driver, telling someone to proceed or get a move on. From the title of a song (1934) by the American songwriter Fred Hillebrand and recorded by Elsie Carlisle in that year and by Hillebrand himself in 1935. The component 'Home, James!' had existed long before – in the works of Thackeray, for example. The choruses of the song are variations on this structure:

> Oh, home James, and don't spare the horses,
> This night has been ruined for me,
> Oh, home James, and don't spare the horses,
> I'm ruined as ruined can be.

(I) hope your rabbit dies. A curse. Mrs D.R. Richards, Essex (1995) sent me first of all what she took to be a toast:

'May your rabbits never die!' which her father used often, and which she assumed he had made up for himself. But, then, while reading her father-in-law's diary of the Empire Cruise of 1923–4, she found that, as a naval officer, he had had to attend a very long and dull party at a big house in Canada. 'It was not possible to get away until 3 a.m.,' Mrs Richards reported, 'by which time he said of his hosts: "I hope all their rabbits die".' Next thing, Mrs Richards was reading Dorothy L. Sayers, *Have His Carcase*, Chap. 7 (1932), in which Lord Peter Wimsey phones Harriet Vane and during the conversation says: 'All right, and I hope your rabbit dies.' So that was it. 'This expression was in current use in my schooldays in the early 1920s and always ended any acrimonious argument or dispute' – anonymous octogenarian (1996).

Many other people responded that they knew the curse in extended versions. 'I first heard it from my husband and his mother who were brought up in the Dewsbury area of Yorkshire. In full, and sounding particularly vindictive, it ran, "Well, all I hope is that his rabbit dies – and he can't sell the hutch"' – Ruth Daughtry, Derbyshire (1996). This same version was heard 'from a Yorkshireman who grew up in Leeds in the 1930s' – Miss Mary Lanning, Bristol (1996). Also sent by Miss D.B. North, West Yorkshire (1996). 'The parting shot after a quarrel was frequently, "I hope yer rabbit dies" but with even more withering scorn went on into "an' yer can't sell t' skin"' – Anne Gledhill, West Yorkshire (1996). 'My mother used to say, "I hope your rabbits die and your rhubarb won't grow" in the 1930s' – Stella Richardson, Essex (1996). 'When I was young (before the war of 1939-45) we used to say, "May your rabbits die and your toenails grow inward for evermore"! This was in Birmingham' – Mrs H.E. Beech, Staffordshire (1997). 'As I am Yorkshire born, I often use the curse even now, but my version is again a different one. I say, "I hope your rabbits die and your white mice turn black"' – Mrs Sylvia Armstrong, Kent (1997).

Stella Gibbons, *Cold Comfort Farm*, Chap. 16 (1932) has her doughty heroine apparently adapt the phrase: '"Then you're a crashing bounder," said Flora, vigorously, "and I hope your water-voles die".'

After much of this had been exposed (and note the strong Yorkshire involvement), Mrs Richards commented (1996): 'It is strange that all the sayings are in the form of curses. My sister and I are again wondering if our father did in fact make up the toast version.' Well, perhaps not: Partridge/*Catch Phrases* has 'May your rabbits flourish!' as a popular farewell (from Australia) since about 1930.

hopeless. See YOU'RE AS DAFT...

horse. See BLIND MAN...; GO AND WATER...; IT'S THE SIGN OF...; LIVE HORSE AND...; LUCK IS OUT WHEN...; NEVER BUY A SADDLE...; WHY BOTHER?...; CAN LEAD...

horse rubbish. Mangled words. Denis Norden admitted in BBC Radio *Quote... Unquote* (21 May 1996) that in his family they have adopted children's sayings, e.g. 'horse rubbish' for horse radish.

horseback. See I DON'T KNOW IF...

horses. See HOME, JAMES...

horses sweat, men perspire – and women merely glow. A saying used to reprove someone who talks of 'sweating'. Casson/Grenfell lists it as a nanny's reprimand in the form: 'Horses sweat, gentlemen perspire, but ladies only gently glow.' J.M. Cohen includes it in *More Comic and Curious Verse* (1956) as merely by Anon, in the form: 'Here's a little proverb that you surely ought to know: / Horses sweat and men perspire, but ladies only glow.'

how many beans make five? A joke riddle, but also uttered as an answer to an impossible question (along the lines of 'how long is a piece of string?' etc). Miss Alice Lloyd was singing a music-hall song in November 1898 which contained these lines:

> You say you've never heard
>   How many beans make five?
> It's time you knew a thing or two –
>   You don't know you're alive!

Miss M.L. King, London SW3, told me (1993) that a/the correct answer is: 'Two in each hand and one in the mouth'. On the other hand: 'Two in each hand, and one up your —' (Wickenden).

how many hundred times have I told you not to exaggerate! In *The Guinness Book of Humorous Irish Anecdotes*, ed. Aubrey Dillon-Malone (1996), this is given with the comment that: 'The Irish penchant for exaggeration is captured in the father's admonition to his son...' But I am not sure it is necessarily an Irish coinage. Compare HAVEN'T I BEEN TELLING YOU...

how much does it cost?/money and fair words. Fobbing-off phrase, reported by the actress Diana Quick on BBC Radio *Quote... Unquote* (20 April 1993).

how true that is, even today. A plonking remark in response to another such. As it turns out, this phrase has a show business origin, but this was by no means clear when I first started investigating it. In 1998, Dr James Atherton noticed my responding to a rather vacuous remark on my radio show with the words, 'How true that is, even today.' He wondered if the phrase came from a sketch or satire upon churchy folk. All I could point to was this from the actor Kenneth Williams's published letters: 'I must say I fell about at your line "Age shall not wither her nor iron bars a cage." I thought "How true that is even today".' This is from a letter dated 2 October 1971. Ian Forsyth, Co. Durham, solved the matter (2000) by urging me to search in three episodes of the BBC Radio show *Round the Horne* (in which Kenneth Williams appeared, of course). Instances of the phrase do indeed occur in the regular parodies of Eamonn Andrews's inept TV chat shows. On 13 and 20 March 1966, Seamus Android (played by Bill Pertwee) replies to one of his guests: 'How true that is even today.' On 27 March, Williams as Claphanger (a movie producer) says, 'You see, I'm illiterate, too.' 'Android' replies: 'Yes. And how true those words are even today.' On 3 April, movie star Zsa Zsa Poltergeist (Betty Marsden) says, 'I'll get around to all of you in time.' Android comments: 'And how true those words are even today.' So we may say that, rather than stemming from the airy philosophising of church folk in the 1960s, the expression is meant to mock the plonking style of a chat-show host. The scripts were written by Barry Took and Marty Feldman.

how's your belly off for spots? [or **how's your belly where the pig bit you?**] Greetings. Fred Goodwin, Shropshire (2000). Partridge/*Catch Phrases* has both of them and dates them from the early 20th century.

hundred. See HOW MANY HUNDRED ... ; IT WILL ALL BE THE SAME ...

hungry. See I'M SO HUNGRY...

hunker. See LESS OF YOUR...

hurry. See HERE'S YOUR HAT...; YOU'LL JUST HAVE TO WAIT...

hurt. See IT WON'T HURT...

husband. See THOUSAND A YEAR OR...

husbands. See THAT'S THE WORST OF THESE...

I

I am speaking to the butcher, not the block. 'When talking to someone who seemed particularly thick or who answered when not being directly addressed, my father would say: "I am speaking to the butcher, not the block". Said I may say in a very good-natured way' – Celia Miller, Essex (1995).

I believe you, thousands wouldn't. Partridge/*Catch Phrases* describes this as 'indicative either of friendship victorious over incredulity or tactfully implying that the addressee is a liar' and finds a citation in R.H. Mottram, *The Spanish Farm* (1927). It is spoken by both the Albert Finney and the Rachel Roberts characters in the film of Alan Sillitoe's *Saturday Night and Sunday Morning* (UK 1960).

I couldn't fancy him if his arse was decked with diamonds. For some reason, I have a note of this expression as having been said by a 'Welsh woman 1920s/30s', but no more.

I don't know if I'm on foot or horseback. I.e. 'I'm flustered.' Source mislaid.

I don't mind if you burn. Once this was the 'smart' rejoinder to the query, 'Do you mind if I smoke?' Another form was 'I don't care if you burst into flame'. The mother of the poet Michael Rosen would reply, nudgingly, 'Before, during or after' (as he recalled on BBC Radio *Quote... Unquote*, 24 May 1994).

'I see', said the blind man (when he couldn't see at all). Partridge/*Catch Phrases* has this from America by the late 19th century, as also, '"I see," said the blind man, as he picked up his hammer and saw."' "I see," said the blind man, "you're a liar," said the dumb' – mother of Stella Richardson, Essex (1998). 'My family had a particular saying from a previous generation for when, after an explanation, "the penny dropped": "'I see,' said the blind man. And do you know what he did? He took up a cup and saucer"' – Martin Tunnicliffe, West Midlands (2000). 'If my mother could not give an answer to a question, she would say, "I see, said the blind man to his dumb and deaf daughter who was blowing steam off cold cabbage"' – Mrs J. Wood, Nottinghamshire (2000).

I want me tea! This was a TV catchphrase but there are still families that consciously repeat it (I belong to one). *The Grove Family* ran on BBC TV 1953–6 and was the forerunner of soap operas like *Coronation Streeet* and *EastEnders*, depicting as it did everyday life in a suburban family. Most memorable was testy old Grandma Grove, played by a wonderful old actress called Nancy Roberts. This was what 'Gran' used to exclaim. Sonia Higgins (2000) recalled that she used to continue: 'I'm faint from lack of nourishment.' In *It's a Great Day!* (UK 1956), a cinema feature, she gets to say, rather, 'Where's me cocoa? I'm faint from lack of nourishment.'

I wasn't born yesterday, you know. Meaning, 'I'm no innocent.' The *OED2* has this as an established saying by 1757. But I can't help feeling its modern use must have been encouraged by the play/film title *Born Yesterday*, Garson Kanin's excellent vehicle for Judy Holliday (1946), about an ignorant girl who wins out in the end.

I will stick your head between your ears. 'I don't know what effect this had on my two sisters and me, but our father used to cow us into obedience with this threat: "If you don't behave yourself at once I will stick your head between your ears"' – Lewis Erlanger, Warwickshire (1997).

I wouldn't fancy him baked. 'If my mother saw what appeared to be a mismatched couple together, she would say, "I don't know what she sees in him – I wouldn't fancy him baked"' – W.S. Hardy, Newton Stewart (1994).

I'll be jiggered! *OED2* has the verb 'to jigger' as a 'vague substitution for a profane oath or imprecation – origin disputed.' Known by 1837. Possibly it has something to do with a slang expression meaning 'to shut up, imprison'.

I'll go out into the garden and eat worms. 'I'll eat humble pie,' often said ironically. An early appearance is in Elsie J. Oxenham, *The Two Form Captains* (1921). The *Sunday Telegraph* (19 March 1989) published a slightly different version: 'Nobody loves me, everybody hates me,/I'll go into the garden and eat worms:/Great big juicy ones, little squiggly-wiggly ones,/Golly, how they wriggles and they squirms.'

(well,) I'll go to the foot of our stairs! An old northern English expression of surprise or amazement – meaning, presumably, that the short walk to the place mentioned would allow the speaker to recover equanimity. Or perhaps it meant it was time to give up and go to bed? Used by Tommy Handley in BBC Radio's *ITMA* (1940s) and elsewhere. Said to have been used by the entertainer George Formby as 'Eeh, I'll go to the foot of our stairs', as also, 'Eeh, I'll go to our 'ouse [pronounced 'our rouse']' – Robina Hinton, Suffolk (1999). Chris Littlefair gave this variation from the North-East (2000): 'I'll go to the bottom of our garden.'

I'll show you the back of my hand. I.e. 'I'll bid you goodbye' or a mock dismissive, as though about to slap or 'show the knuckles to' the other person. Chris Littlefair reported it from the North-East (2000). The version 'Here's the back of my hand to you!' is in Swift's *Polite Conversation* (1738).

I'm chuffed to little apples. 'I'm pleased.' Alison Emmett, London WC1 (1995). 'Chuffed' is famously a Janus word, meaning either 'pleased' or 'displeased', according to context. Partridge/*Slang* does not have this precise example but Paul Beale inserts 'chuffed to (little) naffy [NAAFI]-breaks' from the 1950s/60s.

I'm like Barney's bull, I'm buggered. 'What you say after a hard day's work' – Stella Richardson, Essex (1998). Presumably this refers to the same creature as in the expression listed under ALL BEHIND LIKE...

I'm so hungry, my back is sticking to my front. 'Said by my wife, Diana, who does not claim originality' – Richard Toeman, London N6 (1995). Just as well. There are a number of 'I'm so hungry...' phrases, of which the other nearest to this is: 'I'm so empty, I can feel me backbone touching me belly button.'

I've heard geese fart before in windy weather. 'Whenever I made an extravagant or boastful utterance, my grandmother would say this' – George Goldsmith-Carter, Kent (1989). Another correspondent recalls this as, 'I've heard ducks fart before'.

if a rabbit ran down that, he'd break his neck on the corners. On a crooked parting in the hair (Wickenden).

if I return before I get back, keep me until I arrive... 'A saying of my grandfather's. When going out of the house, he would always turn and say: "I'm leaving now and if I return before I get back, keep me until I arrive." He used this as far back as the First World War, when my father was a young man. I have no idea where my grandfather got this from, but my father started to use it and then, of course, so did I. So four generations of our family have been driven mad by this saying!' – Brian Grist, Surrey (1996).

'If' is a little word with a big meaning. 'A saying of my mother's' – G.R. Brace, Hertfordshire (1998).

if it had been alive it would have bitten you. When something you were looking for is right in front of you (Wickenden).

if it was raining palaces I'd end up with a toilet at the bottom of the garden. The kind of thing said by the terminally miserable/unfortunate/disaster-prone. Myfanwy Talog quoted it on *Quote...Unquote* (16 July 1983). Compare the Australian: 'If it was raining palaces, I'd be hit on the head with the handle of a dunny [privy] door'; 'if it was raining pea soup, I'd only have a fork'; 'if it was raining virgins, I'd end up with a poofter'. Swift's *Polite Conversation* (1738) has: 'Faith, Madam, if it rain'd rich Widows, none of them would fall upon me.' And compare:

if they fell down a sewer they'd come up smelling of roses. On someone always having good luck (Wickenden).

if wishes were horses, beggars would ride. Nannyism (Casson/Grenfell). Or rather a proverb that nannies were once much inclined to quote. In this form, the proverb has been in existence since the 18th century (*CODP*).

if you can't fight, wear a big hat. Partridge/*Catch Phrases* has this as a taunt made to someone who has just bought a new hat. Presumably the implication is that they have bought a big hat, somehow of the type that would intimidate potential opponents. A 1930s starting point is suggested.

if you haven't got your health, you haven't got anything. Informal proverb noted by 1985. Compare the more positive, 'As long as you've got your health, that's the main thing.' Compare also:

if you've got the health and strength to grumble, you're all right. 'My mother, who died recently aged 102, used to say (among much else): "If you've got the health and strength to grumble, you're all right"' – Miss Anna Zaharova, London E11 (1996).

if your father had been a glazier, he'd have fitted you with windows. 'To someone standing between the speaker and a source of light' – Stella Richardson, Essex

(1998). Swift's *Polite Conversation* (1738) has the short version: 'I believe your Father was no Glazier', which Francis Grose, *A Classical Dictionary of the Vulgar Tongue* (1788), glosses: 'If it is answered in the negative, the rejoinder is – I wish he was, that he might make a window through your body to enable us to see the fire or light.' Compare the nannyism in Casson/Grenfell: 'You make a better door than window.'

ignorant as pig-shit and twice as nasty. On someone really hateful: 'They are as ignorant as pig-s--t and twice as nasty' (Wickenden).

ignored. See IT'S BETTER TO HAVE...

improve. See WE DO NOT NECESSARILY...

in and out – like a dog at a fair. The mother of Max Stafford-Clark, the theatre director, came from Nottinghamshire and 'kept a very clean house', as he put it on BBC Radio *Quote...Unquote* (18 May 1993). 'We used to have to take our shoes off when we came in the door, if she'd done the cleaning that day. If we'd been in and out of the back door more than twice in a morning, she would say, "Either in or out – you're like a dog at a fair".' Max wondered if this was a local expression. Well, his mother was not alone in using it and, in fact, it also happens to be a *quotation* from R.H. Barham's poem 'The Jackdaw of Rheims', published with *The Ingoldsby Legends* in 1840. The eponymous bird busies itself on the Cardinal's table:

> In and out
> Through the motley rout,
> That little jackdaw kept hopping about:
> Here and there,

> Like a dog at a fair,
> Over comfits and cates [dainties],
> And dishes and plates...

Barham seems, however, to have been using an already established expression. Apperson finds 'As sprites in the haire, Or dogges in the ffayre' by 1520. In 1893, G.L. Gower's *Glossary of Surrey Words* had the version: 'They didn't keep nothing reg'lar, it was all over the place like a dog at a fair.'

in days of old and knights were bold and monkeys chewed tobacco. A promising start to a story which does not, however, materialise. Mother of Marjorie Wild, Devon (2000). I seem to recall from my youth a somewhat frisky rhyme beginning, 'In days of old when knights were bold...' – but can't remember whatever happened after that.

'Indigestion is the Question,' said the Bunnies Brown/'As to whether We shall ever Get to London Town.' Rhyme remembered by Jim Snell, Sussex (1998) as being spoken by his mother in about 1918.

ins and outs of a Merryman's backside. 'When confronted by any complicated form to be filled in, my mother would remark that the inquirer wanted to know "The ins and outs of a Merryman's backside". This rather unrefined expression became general in the family' – Rose Shipton, Gloucestershire (1994). The Merryman here is as in the sense of jester or buffoon, defined by Francis Grose's *Dictionary of the Vulgar Tongue* (1785) as: 'Merry Andrew, or Mr. Merryman, the jack pudding, jester, or zany of a mountebank, usually dressed in a party coloured coat.'

Compare WANTS TO KNOW THE INS AND OUTS OF A NAG'S ARSE.

inspect. See GO AND CHECK THE PLUMBING.

it *do*, don't it. 'In the 1920s, my grandparents took a lodger from Norfolk whose favourite expression was, "It *do*, don't it?" One year, our family took a holiday in Cromer and, on arrival, mother made a remark about the weather to our landlady, who replied: "It *don't*, do it?" This riposte has lived on in our family' – Daphne Ibbott, Herefordshire (2000). One might compare 'One never knows, do one?', a phrase always associated with the jazz pianist Fats Waller. He seems to have said it on a number of occasions and also in the film *Stormy Weather* in 1943, the year he died. But it is also the title of a song written by Harry Revel and Mack Gordon for a film called *Stowaway* which came earlier in 1936. And that was a song that was sung later by Billie Holiday. Waller speaks the phrase at the end of his recording of 'Your Feet's Too Big' (1939).

it fits like a stocking on a chicken's lip. I.e. 'No damn good, it doesn't fit at all'. 'My Yorkshire mother-in-law would say this if an article of clothing was badly made' – Mrs Phyllis Jessop, Hampshire (1993). Paul Beale glossed this as 'a traditional carpenter's catchphrase which I first heard from a Loughborough College carpenter and joiner in 1990.'

it shone like a tanner on a sweep's arse. 'A Cockney cousin of mine once told me of her pleasure at receiving, from her husband, the gift of a baby grand piano. She described the beautiful lustre of the instrument with these words' – Peter Foulds, Co. Durham (1992). Partridge/ *Slang* has 'shine like a shilling up a sweep's arse' – which is a touch more alliterative – and dates it 'early C20'.

it will all be the same in a hundred years' time. Professor Richard L. Gregory remembered that this is what his mother would respond when, as a little boy, he said anything silly. Now, he disapproves of this check on originality (as he explained on BBC Radio *Quote... Unquote*, 26 April 1994). It is a quite widely-known put down and as 'It will all be one in a hundred/thousand years', it was recorded in various versions between 1611 and 1839. Swift's *Polite Conversation* (1738) has: 'My Comfort is, it will be all one a thousand Years hence.' Ralph Waldo Emerson, *Representative Men*, 'Montaigne; or The Skeptic' (1850) has: 'Keep cool: it will be all one a hundred years hence.' Bill Wilkes told Paul Beale (1994) that his mother, originally from Norfolk, used the expression 'by that time you'll all be dead and your arse cold' in the same sense.

Compare Samuel Johnson's excellent advice for putting a distressful situation in perspective: 'Consider, Sir, how insignificant this will appear a twelvemonth hence' (Boswell's *Life of Johnson*, for 6 July 1763).

it will be a covering. 'My husband's mother was a very talented dressmaker/tailoress whose services were much in demand. She occasionally made an outfit for her sister who, at the final fitting, would often pay her the compliment, "Oh, well, it'll be a covering"' – Lynne Carter, Buckinghamshire (1996).

it will turn up on your own doorstep. 'If you were angry and wished someone bad luck: "Don't say that, it will turn up on your own doorstep"' (Wickenden).

it won't hurt – where there's no sense there's no feeling. 'Of a bump on the head' – Stella Richardson, Essex (1998).

it'd be a blessing if the Lord called him/her. 'Of a hypochondriacal old person' – Stella Richardson, Essex (1998).

it'll either rain or go dark before morning. 'Into a silence – and apropos of nothing – would drop this gem' – Stella Richardson, Essex (1998).

it'll never get well if you pick it. 'The phrase which my father (1892–1988) always quoted if he saw someone scratching at a spot or scab was, "Remember the words that our brave Nelson said, it'll never get well if you pick it" said in a sort of sing-song rhythmic fashion as though they were words from a song or poem' – Douglas Linnington, Surrey (1998). A nannyism in Casson/ Grenfell.

it's a monkey's wedding. This is a 20th century African catchphrase, 'applied to weather characterised by a drizzling rain accompanied by a shining sun' – Partridge/ *Catch Phrases*, known by 1968. Compare the American saying, for the same eventuality, 'The Devil is beating his wife' (by ?1900). And compare 'A fox's wedding and a monkey's dance' – used when it starts to rain but the sun continues to shine and first heard in a military boarding school at Sanawar, India, by Grace Constable (2000). Partridge/*Slang* also has 'monkey's wedding' as a naval term for an unpleasant smell. Given that foxes are also noted for their smell, could there be something to do with smell of damp ground warmed by sun going on here? There have been other attempts to describe this phenomenon. Apperson dates from 1666 the proverbial expression 'When it rains and the sun shines at the same time the devil is beating his wife.' Or 'is beating his grandmother...he is laughing and she is crying.'

it's a poor house which can't afford one lady. 'My Irish mother, when I was reading when I knew I should be helping in the house' – Kate Cunningham, Hampshire (2000).

it's all in the family. *All In the Family* was the title of the American TV version (from 1971) of the BBC's sitcom *Till Death Us Do Part*. The respective main characters were Archie Bunker and Alf Garnett, racists and bigots both. But what of the American title? It is not a phrase much known elsewhere. The implication would seem to be '... so there's no need to be over-punctilious, stand on ceremony, or fuss too much about obligations' (often with an ironical tinge). Compare 'we are all friends here!'

There is not a trace of the phrase in the *OED2*. However, there is an 1874 citation 'all *outside* the family, tribe or nation were usually held as enemies', which may hint at the possible existence of an opposite construction.

The phrase does occur in Chapter 21, 'Going Aboard', of Herman Melville's *Moby Dick* (1851) – emphasising a likely American origin. Elijah is trying to warn Ishmael and Queequeg against the *Pequod* and its captain: '"Morning to ye! morning to ye!" he rejoined, again moving off. "Oh! I was going to warn ye against – but never mind, never mind – it's all one, all in the family too; – sharp frost this morning, ain't it? Good bye to ye. Shan't see ye again very soon, I guess; unless it's before the Grand Jury".'

it's better to have your tail pulled than to be ignored. 'This was a saying often heard in our house. It could be attributed, if he could have talked, to an affectionate but eccentric cat we once had' – R.J. Watkins, Cleveland (1994).

it's dark/black over Bill's/Will's mother's way... Paul Beale in his revision of Partridge/*Catch Phrases* mentions the expression 'it's a bit black over *Bill's* mother's', referring to the weather, when rain threatens, and gives an East Midlands source. H.S. Middleton, Shropshire, formerly of Leicestershire, and whose brother was called Bill, wrote in 1993 to say how, in the early 1920s, a certain Len Moss had looked through the sitting room window in the direction of Mr Middleton's home and said, 'It looks black over Bill's mother's.' Was this the origin of the phrase (which sometimes occurs elsewhere as 'over *Will's* mother's way')?

All I was able to tell Mr Middleton was that in 1930, the erudite journal *Notes and Queries* carried a query about this phrase in the form 'it looks pretty black over Will's Mother's'. It was described as an 'old Sussex' saying. And there was no response. Barry Day of New York, NY, recalled that 'It's a bit black over Bill's mother's' used to be said a great deal by *his* mother when he was growing up in Derbyshire. 'It was always said ironically,' he added. 'So I can confirm its Midlands usage.'

I first heard about it on a London radio phone-in (June 1990), in the form 'It looks like rain...over Will's mother's way.' In *Verbatim* (Autumn 1993), Alan Major discussed a number of 'Kentish sayings' and included, 'Out Will's mother's way', meaning 'somewhere else, in the distance, on the horizon'. Major added 'Who Will's mother was is unknown, but there are several similar expressions, with word variations, used in other English counties. In Gloucestershire, the expression is "It's dark over our Bill's Mum's mind".'

The Revd P.W. Gallup, Hampshire, wrote in 1994 that he had traced the saying in eleven counties and commented on its age: 'I have friends in their late eighties who as children knew it well from their parents and say that it was then widely known and used. This suggests that the saying has been used at least by several generations.' Since 1993, I have received a goodly number of claims from correspondents that they were personally acquainted with the original Bill and his mother.

it's enough to make a parson swear. 'I recall members of my family saying this after some aggravation' – Colleen Spittles, Kent (1993). Indeed, it is a well-known expression and quite old. Edward Ward used it in *Hudibras Redivivus* (1706): 'Your Folly makes me stare;/Such talk would make a Parson swear', and it appears in Swift's *Polite Conversation* (1738). 'My father, who never used strong language, in spite of having been in the Navy, used to say such things as "Damn and set fire to it" and "It's enough to make a parson swear and burn his books"' – Janet C. Egan, Middlesex (2000).

It's not the cough that carries you off/It's the coffin they carry you off in. 'My husband's mother used to say this' – Mrs M. Jones, West Midlands (1995). 'In my boyhood, my elderly uncle Ed from Essex, with whom I lived for several years just after the war, had a stock comment, "It wasn't the cough that carried him off, it was the coffin they carried him off in"' – Robert Priddy, Nesoddtangen, Norway (1998). 'Used whenever someone has a coughing fit' – Marian Horner, Cambridgeshire (1998). Iona and Peter Opie include this in *The Lore and Language of Schoolchildren* (1959) as a type of ghoulish catchphrase enjoyed by ten-year-olds.

But where does it come from? When I heard Billy Cotton's recording of Alan Breeze singing 'It Ain't the Cough' (written by Mann, about 1956), I made the assumption that this was based on some earlier song, but that it might lead us to the true original. In time, I obtained the music of a comic song called 'The Cough-Drop Shop' written by Leslie Sarony in 1932. It ends:

> When you get to the cough-drop shop,
> Remember when you're coughing,
> It's not the cough that carries you off,
> It's the coffin they carry you off in!

William Crowe, meanwhile, very definitely recalls hearing the last line in 1927, so perhaps both songs are borrowing from something even earlier.

it's nourishment I want, not punishment. 'Said by a Lancastrian woman in her eighties, when asked why she had not remarried' – according to the historian Michael Wood on BBC Radio *Quote...Unquote* (13 July 1985). A letter dated 20 October 1969 from the actor Kenneth Williams, commiserating on the death of a friend's mother, contains this: 'Mine is still going strong, and leaves on the 25th for a cruise in the Med. I told her to be careful "Keep your hand on your ha'penny dear" I said, "they're all after a bit out there" and she retorted "Don't worry yourself, I want nourishment, not punishment" so I think she knows what she's doing. Certainly at 69 she ought to...' – from *The Kenneth Williams Letters* (1994).

it's snowing in Paris. 'Meaning that your petticoat is showing below your skirt' – Gisela Lehmann, Herefordshire (1995). Iona and Peter Opie include this in *The Lore* *and Language of Schoolchildren* (1959) as a 'juvenile corrective', along with 'S.O.S.' (Slip On Show) and 'Is your name Seymour?' To which one might add another, 'It's snowing down South'.

(oh well,) it's the last Tuesday [or whatever day it is] **of the week...** 'On considering whether to accept a treat' – John G. Dudderidge, Bedfordshire (1995).

it's the sign of a hard winter when the hay runs after the horse. Informal proverb (or, possibly, a once-only utterance). From Arnold Bennett, *The Journals* (1971): 'Thursday, 10 August [1899] – I have just remembered a saying of Mrs Drummer, our new housekeeper at Witley. She said to me: "There's a lot of old maids in the village, sir, as wants men. There was three of 'em after a curate as we had here, a very nice young gentleman he was, sir. No matter how often the church was opened those women would be there, sir, even if it was five times a day. It's a sign of a hard winter, sir, when the hay begins to run after the horse.'

Compare these similar proverbs from John Ray's collection (1678): 'It's time to set when the oven comes to the dough' and 'It's time to yoke when the cart comes to the caples [horses].'

J

jackass. See SHORT AND SWEET LIKE A...

Jacob's join. In 1997, Donald H. Stock, having pursued the matter in and around Lytham, Lancashire, without success, asked about this expression to describe a gathering where everyone brings along an item of food or drink. Partridge/*Slang* states that it was gathered from a Lancashire source also and defines it as, 'What is sometimes called a "faith supper" in church circles, i.e. the eating equivalent of a bottle party, each participant making a contribution to the communal meal.' What the connection is with the biblical Jacob, if any, is not clear. Mr Stock later noted that he had heard of the phrase 'American pie' being applied to the same sort of gathering. Can this be so?

jam. See OH LOOK, MAMA...

James. See HOME, JAMES...

jelly. See CAN I PRESS...

Jemima. See WHOOPS, JEMIMA!

jiggered. See I'LL BE...

job. See GO TO DO A JOB...

Joe Egg. See SIT ABOUT LIKE JOE EGG...

Johnny, get your gun, there's a cow in the garden. 'My maternal grandfather, a lovely man, used to chant this to his small grandchildren. While the first four words are part of a patriotic American First World War song, I've never been able to establish whether the remainder was his own, invented to amuse us, or also a quotation' – Mary B. Maggs, Conwy (1998). Yes, 'Johnny, Get Your Gun' was written in 1886 and eventually inspired Irving Berlin with the title for *Annie Get Your Gun*, but the remainder seems to be original. Compare, however, PARDON, MRS ARDEN...

joined. See GO AND SEE THE MAN...

joints. See ALL JOINTS...

joke over. 'If no one laughed at his or other passing jokes, my uncle would slip this in with quick resignation' – Robert Priddy, Nesoddtangen, Norway (1998). According to Roger Wilmut, *Kindly Leave the Stage!* (1985), the Yorkshire comedian Dick Henderson had a sort of catchphrase in his act when he would say, 'Ha! Ha! – joke over', at the conclusion of an obvious joke.

jug. See TELL HIM TO STICK IT UP...

just in time; or, born in the vestry! 'When someone is late' – recalled by Antony Jay on BBC Radio *Quote...Unquote*

(29 March 1994). Partridge / *Catch Phrases* notes: 'Obviously, applied [and referring] to a wedding held only just in time to prevent the coming child from being adjudged illegitimate.' Paul Beale adds: 'Perhaps modelled on typical Victorian novel-titles.'

just think, if we lived here, we'd be home by now. Sandi Toksvig's father was a journalist and they were always travelling, especially in the US. After driving all day he would say, 'Just think, if we lived here, we'd be home now' – as Sandi recalled on BBC Radio *Quote... Unquote* (21 May 1996).

K

(that should) keep body and soul together. 'In my late husband's family, a great saying when serving up a substantial snack or full meal was, "There you are, that will keep B. and S. Tog'" – Joan Bell, Clackmannanshire (1992). 'Keeping body [*or* life] and soul together' is, of course, an old phrase. According to the *OED2*, 'Tate' in Dryden's *Juvenal* (1697) has: 'The Vascons once with Man's Flesh (as 'tis sed)/Kept Life and Soul together'. Jane Collier, *The Art of Tormenting* (1753) has: 'By never letting him see you swallow half enough to keep body and soul together.' *The Century Illustrated Monthly Magazine* (November 1884) has: 'How on earth they managed to keep body and soul together.'

keep it dark and I'll buy you a lantern. 'If my mother told me something she didn't wish me to disclose to anyone else, she would say: "Keep it dark and I'll buy you a lantern'" – Mrs J. Tunnicliff, Worcestershire (1995). 'Keep it dark!', on its own, has an interesting history. The basic expression, meaning 'keep it secret', had been in use by 1681. Then it became a security slogan during the Second World War (in the UK) and appeared in more than one formulation, also in verse:

If you've news of our munitions
> KEEP IT DARK

Ships or plans or troop positions
> KEEP IT DARK

Lives are lost through conversation
Here's a tip for the duration
When you've private information.
> KEEP IT DARK.

Shush, Keep It Dark was the title of a variety show running in London during September 1940. Later, the naval version of the BBC radio show *Merry Go Round* (1943–8) featured a character called Commander High-Price (Jon Pertwee) whose catchphrase was, 'Hush, keep it dark!'

None of this had been forgotten by 1983, apparently, when Anthony Beaumont-Dark, a Tory candidate in the General Election, campaigned successfully for re-election with the slogan, 'Keep it Dark'.

kettle. See AS MUCH USE AS ...

king. See OH KING, LIVE FOREVER ... ; TRUE, O KING!

kings. See GO WHERE KINGS ...

kipper. See HANG THE EXPENSE ...

kippers. See ALL CURTAINS ...

kissed. See EVERYBODY TO THEIR ...

knickers. See ALL FUR COAT ... ; GET YOUR HAT ... ; WHAT'S THE TIME ...

knife-box. See BACK IN THE ...

knights. See IN DAYS OF OLD ...

knobs. See SAME TO YOU WITH BRASS ...

knobs and chairs and pump-handles. Fobbing-off phrase.
'This was my mother's reply to our daily demands of
"What's for dinner, Mum?" The vision of this has always
fascinated me. Mum said her father always used to say it'
– Ms J. Harrison, Powys (1994). Compare 'A rasher of wind
and a fried snowball' – a nannyism (in answer to the
question 'What's for lunch?') in Casson/Grenfell.

knocker. See AS BLACK...; LET THEM TAKE IT OUT...

knot. See TIE THAT KNOT WITH YOUR TONGUE...

know. See FORGOTTEN MORE...; THAT'S FOR ME TO KNOW...

L

lace. See LIVER WITH LACE...

laces. See THERE ARE THREE SORTS OF...

lady. See IT'S A POOR HOUSE...

language. See GOLD COIN SPEAKS...

lantern. See KEEP IT DARK...

larovers for meddlers and crutches for lame ducks.
Fobbing-off phrase – and like all such, this is a way of not
giving an answer to an inquisitive person, especially a
child. If someone asks, 'What have you got there?' this is
the reply. Possibly a Northern dialect expression originally,
but now quite widespread. Could 'meddlers' be 'medlars'
(i.e. the fruit – also a term for the female genitals, as it
happens)?

Philip N. Wicks, Northamptonshire, recalled (1994):
'When as a small child I asked my Mother [who hailed
from Norfolk], "What's in there?" regarding the contents
of any unreadable packet or blank blue grocer's bag, she
would reply secretively, "Leerooks for meddlers and beans

for gooses eyes". I've wondered for 40 years what she meant.'

Partridge/*Catch Phrases* finds a version already in use by 1668. Apperson explained 'larovers' as 'lay-overs' – things laid over, covered up, to protect them from meddlers – and concluded: 'Almost every county has its variation probably of this phrase. The most common form in which it survives, however, is "Layers for meddler".' A surprising occurrence is in Chapter 32 of Margaret Mitchell's *Gone With the Wind* (1936). Scarlett O'Hara, when asked who, in Atlanta, is going to lend her money that she needs to pay the taxes on Tara, avoids answering the question by saying, 'archly': 'Layovers catch meddlers.'

Another explanation is that 'lay-holes for medlars' are what you put the fruit in to ripen. Partridge also gives the variant: 'Crutches for meddlers and legs for lame ducks'. No easy solution to this one. Compare WHIMWAM FOR A GOOSE'S BRIDLE.

last. See IT'S THE LAST...

late. See TOO LATE, TOO LATE...; YOU'D BE LATE...

laugh. See DON'T MAKE ME...; LOUD LAUGH DENOTES...

laughing always comes to crying. Proverb. From Peter Nichols, *Forget-Me-Not-Lane*, Act 2 (1971): 'Still – laughing always comes to crying, as my mother would say, and all this joy led to a hasty scene at the registry office.'

laughs. See SO MISERABLE THAT...

Laurence. See LAZY LARRENCE.

lazy. See AS LAZY...

lazy Larrence/Laurence/Lawrence. 'One of my father's sayings if we said we were too tired to do anything was "You've got Laurence"' – Mrs K.Y. Williams, Herefordshire (1998). This dates back to 1650, by some accounts. The reference may be to the general 'heat around St Lawrence's day (10 August) or to the legend of the martyred St Lawrence being too lazy to move in the flames' – according to Apperson and Partridge/*Slang*.

Leather Arse. See THERE NEVER WERE SUCH TIMES...

leg. See GET OFF MY...; GOT A BONE...

legs. See BETTER LEGS...; YOU COULD ARGUE/TALK...

lemon. See ANSWER'S A LEMON.

less of your hunker sliding. 'My mother, who was born on Tyneside, would say when her children were "playing for time", "less of your hunker sliding." Apparently North East miners call their haunches, "hunkers"' – Mrs S.F. Cooper, Co. Durham (1995).

let the dog see the rabbit. 'Said to others when crowding around a fire' – Stella Richardson, Essex (1998). Partridge/ *Catch Phrases* gives a less specific meaning – 'get out of the way, get out of the light', from dog-track frequenters.

let them take it out on the knockers. 'On unwelcome visitors at the door' (Wickenden).

let your finger touch your ear, and they'll bite their tongue. 'If you said, "Someone is talking about me, my ear is burning", Mum would say this' (Wickenden).

let your meat stop your mouth. 'My grandfather kept me quiet during family mealtimes when I was a child with the words, "Let your meat stop your mouth", advice which was apparently given to him by his own grandfather many years before' – Emma Hodgson, Co. Durham (letter in the *Independent*, 10 August 1994).

let's go so that we can come home. 'One of my aunts – a somewhat lugubrious woman with a strong sense of duty – would always say this when setting off on a visit from which there was little expectation of pleasure. In childhood I thought it slightly absurd. Fifty or so years on, I find myself saying exactly the same thing!' – Guinevere Ventress, Cambridgeshire (1995).

let's have a cup of tea and a fag and forget our troubles. 'When you were troubled' (Wickenden).

let's not, and say we did! 'While my father would never encourage me to lie, when confronted with something relatively trivial he did not want to do, he would say this' – Richard Paul-Jones, East Sussex (2000). Partridge/*Catch Phrases* has it as American, mainly juvenile, from about 1925 and 'probably long extinct'.

letter. See Y'S A CROOKED LETTER.

liar. See YOU ARE A BIGGER . . .

(to give something a) lick and a promise. 'On hasty cleaning (of the body)' (Wickenden).

(that) licks hen racing. 'My mother aged 90 has a saying. If anything puzzles her – such as mislaying something she had recently handled – she will look round, then stop and say, "Well, that licks hen racing"' – Mrs Gwyneth Harwood, North Yorkshire (1995), who later wrote to say that there had been a Radio 4 talk by Les Woodland on 'one man's efforts to revive the old country tradition of chicken racing' – apparently in Norfolk. A leg pull? 'My mother had a fund of sayings. About anything surprising, she would say: "That caps hen-racing"' – Ethel S. Dowey, North Yorkshire.

life. See ANYTHING FOR A QUIET . . . ; THERE'S LIFE . . .

life is hard. This stern text was always quoted to Peter Wood, the theatre director, by what he called his West Country 'Protestant Work Ethic' family. Many years later, he was struggling upstairs with his parrot, Sid, in his cage – when the parrot, too, suddenly said it to him, as he recalled on BBC Radio *Quote . . . Unquote* (31 March 1992).

Other forms of this exclamation would include the traditional: 'It's a hard life', 'Life is hell', 'Life is not a bed of roses', 'Life wasn't meant to be easy', 'Life is unfair'.

light. See TOO LIGHT . . .

(you are) like a cow with a musket. 'When one was being awkward in some task' – Miss O.E. Burns, West Midlands (1995). 'As awkward as a cow with a musket' – Andrew Craton, Hampshire (1999).

like a donkey eats strawberries. My mother-in-law – or so I am reliably informed by someone better placed to know – used to say this when describing how someone was extremely enthusiastic about something (and not just food). She came from Buckinghamshire and it may be a local expression.

like a Drury Lane fairy. 'I'm 70 years old and was brought up by a grandmother who in turn was brought up by a mother who took in washing at the back of Leicester Square. When I came home crying because I'd fallen over and hurt myself, my grandmother always said, "You're like a Drury Lane fairy – always in trouble." She would never tell me what a Drury Lane fairy was...' – Violet Mills, West Sussex (1994).

Understandably. J. Redding Ware's *Passing English of the Victorian Era* (1909) defines a 'fairy' as 'a debauched, hideous old woman, especially when drunk'. Francis Grose's *Dictionary of the Vulgar Tongue* (1785) has 'Drury Lane vestal' = 'harlot'. 'My family always said, "You sound just like a Drury Lane dressmaker" to anyone complaining of various aches and pains, usually trivialities. Sometimes combined with the maladies there would be a moan about their general life' – Mrs B. Parker, Bedfordshire (2000).

like a fart in a colander. 'Dithering' (Wickenden) or 'rushing around'. Partridge/*Catch Phrases* suggests an origin sometime in the 1920s. This is also used when describing someone particularly evasive or slippery. I was first introduced to this wonderful expression by Roy Hudd (on BBC Radio *Quote...Unquote*, 24 May 1994). Although I found it hugely amusing, I did not quite understand the mechanics of it until Mrs J. Harrison, Powys, wrote that, as she knew it, the phrase was used to describe someone who was indecisive and the complete version was: 'He's like a fart in a colander – can't make up his mind which hole to come out of!'

A slightly different version of the same idea: 'My own grandmother used a wealth of descriptive and colourful expressions. One frequently addressed to me was, "Can't you just sit still, child, fidgetting about like a parched pea in a colander!"' – Mrs Stella Mummery, London SW14 (1995).

like a ferret down a rabbit hole. 'An opportunist: "He was in there like a ferret down a rabbit hole"' (Wickenden).

like a parish oven. 'According to my mother, a large mouth was "like a parish oven"' – Mrs Jean Wigget, Kent (1995).

like a streak of tap water dressed up. 'Of a thin man' – Stella Richardson, Essex (1998). Compare FACE LIKE A YARD OF PUMP-WATER.

like an angel with pit clogs on. 'My mother came from a small village in Lancashire and her sayings really have to be heard in her accent. Speaking of someone who thought themselves a cut above everyone else: "He/she is like an angel with pit clogs on" – Margaret Rowden, Somerset (1998).

like an old woman with a worsted leg. 'As a child, if I was making a clumsy effort at carrying out a simple task, my father (who came from Aberdeen) would say: "You're like an old woman with a worsted leg"' – Andrew G. Forsyth, Hertfordshire (1996). 'When I was young, 80 years ago, I lived with my grandmother on the Suffolk coast at Aldeburgh. When I did anything silly or inept she would say, "You are like the man on the beach with a worsted nose who has never seen the sea"' – George Goldsmith-Carter, Kent (1989). So, what is this with 'worsted'? See also WHAT A WORLD IT IS FOR WOOSSIT...

like Billy Gibbons' cat, you will know all about it. 'If one had misbehaved, the usual reprimand from my mother would be, "If you do that again, you will be like Gibbons' cat, you will know all about it"' – Marjorie E. Weston, West Sussex (1998).

like the barber's cat – full of wind and water. 'When trying to reinforce an argument with "so and so said", this was the reply (if a male was quoted), ("water" to rhyme with "hatter")' – Margaret Martin, Surrey (1993). Partridge/*Slang* has 'like the barber's cat – all wind and piss', and dates it from the late 19th century. John Beaumont, Hertfordshire (2000) added that his grandfather used to say after a good Sunday dinner, 'I'm full of wind and water like a barber's cat.' This was around the time of the Second World War.

like the colour of Old Nick's nutting bag. 'Dirty hands looked "like the colour of Old Nick's nutting bag"' – mother of Mrs Jean Wigget, Kent (1995). This is remembered elsewhere as 'You're black as the Devil's nutting bag'. Apperson has it by 1866.

like when pussy burns her backside on a snowball. 'On something improbable' (Wickenden).

liking. See EVERYBODY TO THEIR...

lilies. See GO AND WATER THE LILIES.

lip. See DON'T MAKE ME...; IT FITS LIKE...; RIDE TO...

lips. See MOMENT ON YOUR LIPS...

little. See EVERY LITTLE...

(a) little older than my teeth and as old as my tongue. Nannyism (Casson/Grenfell). What nannies should reply, when asked their age by inquisitive young persons. Jonathan Swift had it in *Polite Conversation* by 1738 as, 'Why, I am as old as my Tongue, and a little older than my teeth'.

little pitchers have big ears. 'A warning that children are around [who may hear what they should not]' – friend of Marjorie Wild, Devon (2000). Apperson finds this in Heywood's *Proverbs* (1546), as: 'Auoyd your children: small pitchers have wide eares.' Casson/Grenfell has the nannyism: 'Little pitchers have long ears, so have donkeys.'

little things please little minds. Apperson finds this in Lyly's *Sapho and Phao* (1584), with 'catch' for 'please'. The actress June Whitfield, quoting this on BBC Radio *Quote... Unquote* (13 June 1995), added: 'Little trousers fit little behinds.'

live horse and you'll eat corn. 'When I told my Mum I'd repay her in a couple of days for the tights/perfume/whatever I'd "borrowed", she'd say (wryly, I now know): "Och aye, live horse and you'll eat corn"' – Morag Becker, London SE22 (1996). Presumably derived from:

live horse and you'll get grass. Apperson has, rather, 'Live, horse! And thou shalt have grass' and finds it, in that form, in Swift's *Polite Conversation* (1738). Partridge/*Slang* glosses it as, 'Well, let's wait and see! Later on, we'll see!'

liver with lace holes in. Fobbing-off phrase. 'In answer to the question, "What's for tea?"' – Margaret Rowden, Somerset (1995).

loaf. See SLICE OFF A CUT LOAF...

(the) longest mile is the last mile home. 'After a long walk' (Wickenden).

look. See THERE'S ONLY ONE LOOK...

look for one thing and you'll find another. 'If you lost something (and you know what? You often did too!)' (Wickenden).

(you) look like you've lost a shilling and found a tanner. 'My late father used this saying if he saw an old friend who looked a bit down in the mouth' – Arthur W. Jillions, Essex (1995). 'You look as though you've lost a bob and found a tanner' – father of E.N. Rouse, Worcestershire (2000). A bob/shilling was worth twice a tanner/sixpence, hence the disappointment. This has probably derived from the earlier sayings around the name of John Toy (as in *Cornish Proverbs*, 1864). C.H. Spurgeon, *Ploughman's Pictures* (1880) has: 'The luck that comes to them is like Johnny Toy's, who lost a shilling and found a two-penny loaf.'

(I'll) look over your heads and see your nose. 'My Yorkshire mother used to say "if you don't behave, I'll look over your heads and see your nose". I never understood this, but it always had the desired effect!' – Jean Findlay, Northumberland (1996).

looked like they had been drinking vinegar off a fork. 'My grandmother, who looked like a cross between Golda Meir and Peter Ustinov, used to say this of people with particularly sour faces' – Helen Christmas, Cardiff (2000). Partridge/*Slang* has this from the mid-19th century.

looking. See WHAT ARE YOU...

looks. See CAN'T HELP...

lop. See SKIN A LOP FOR...

Lord. See IT'D BE A BLESSING...

lost. See YOU'LL NEVER GET LOST...

(a) loud laugh denotes the vacant mind. Informal proverb. Mother of Mrs Jean Wigget, Kent (1995).

lovely weather for ducks! What you say when it is raining. Although it must be ancient, I have not found a citation in this precise form before 1985. Partridge/*Catch Phrases* finds 'nice weather for ducks' in Philip Oakes, *Experiment at Proto* (1973). Apperson has 'Weather meete to sette paddockes [frogs] abroode in' from Heywood's *Proverbs* (1546) and 'another fine week for the ducks' in Charles Dickens, *The Old Curiosity Shop*, Chap. 2 (1840). He also suggests that the predominant form is 'fine weather for ducks'.

lower. See GO AND LOWER...

(you know your) luck is out when a blind horse kicks you. (Wickenden).

Ludlum. See AS LAZY...

M

M.I.K. (More In Kitchen). Initial code. In other words, 'Go ahead and eat it'. Partridge/*Slang* has this by 1939.

mackerel. See SPRAT TO CATCH A ...

(a) mackerel sky is very wet – or very dry. The actress Sian Phillips chose this to illustrate the unhelpfulness of weather proverbs (on BBC Radio *Quote...Unquote*, 13 April 1993). Mrs Barbara Williams, Plymouth, wrote (1993) that the version she grew up with was, 'Mackerel sky, mackerel sky/Neither wet, neither dry.' Apperson finds any number of explanations as to what a mackerel sky foretells and none of them is very helpful. For example, from West Somerset (1886): 'Mackerel-sky! not much wet, not much dry.'

mad. See ALL OVER...; THEY'RE ALL MAD BUT ME AND THEE...

(I) made it up out of my own head. 'My mother, an inspired cook, if asked the source of a particular recipe would invariably reply, "I made it up out of my own head and there are plenty of ingredients left"' – Kenneth F. Buckingham, Surrey (1995).

maggot. See TAKE THE MAGGOT FOR...; WHAT'S WORSE THAN EATING...

major. See GO AND PARTAKE OF...

make a noise quietly. 'As children we were told to "make a noise quietly"' – Mrs D.M Broom, Berkshire (1996).

makes. See AS HE MAKES...

man. See GO AND SEE A...

(a) man convinced against his will is of the same opinion still. Proverb. 'I once heard in a North Staffordshire pub an expression which was common in the area and used by a mother telling off one of her children for trying to bully another into doing something he did not want to do' – John Bridge, Kent (1995). The earliest appearance of this proverb (and very likely the origin) would seem to be in Samuel Butler, *Hudibras* (1678): 'He that complies against his Will,/Is of his own Opinion still;/Which he may adhere to, yet disown,/For reasons to himself best known.'

Man is as God made him. Proverb. From Henry Reed, *The Primal Scene, As It Were...* (1958): [On the horribleness of kellyfish] 'They are as God made them, Mr Reeve.' From Swift, *Polite Conversation* (1738): 'My Lord, I am as God made me.' Alas, I have not been able to find earlier examples of this view – which must be ancient because we have: 'Every man is as God made him, and often even worse [*Cada uno es como Dios le hizo, y aun peor muchas veces*]' – Miguel de Cervantes, *Don Quixote*, Pt 2, Chap. 4 (1615). Sancho Panza's comment.

manners. See WE SHALL HAVE TO EKE IT OUT...

(it's as rare as) manners amongst tanners and the Grace of God amongst sinners. 'If my Irish Grandmother didn't believe something (e.g. my saying "I'll do the washing up"), she would sarcastically say this' – Peter Hammond, Hertfordshire (2000).

many years ago... An introductory phrase from Denis Norden's list of old person's phrases (on BBC Radio *Quote...Unquote*, 21 May 1996).

match. See HAVE YOU GOT A...

matches. See AS HE MAKES...

may you never meet a mouse in your pantry with tears in his eyes. Presumably the wish here is that your cupboard never be bare. 'A saying of my late grandfather' – John O'Byrne, Dublin (1998).

meadow. See END UP IN...

meal. See THAT'S ANOTHER MEAL...

mean. See SO MEAN SHE WOULDN'T GIVE...

meat. See LET YOUR MEAT STOP...

meddlers. See LAROVERS FOR MEDDLERS...

Meredith, we're in! This catchphrase originated as a shout of triumph in a music-hall sketch called 'The Bailiff' (or 'Moses and Son') but has certainly passed into many a household's usage. It was uttered by Fred Kitchen (1872–1950), the leading comedian with Fred Karno's company. The sketch was first seen about 1907, and the phrase was used each time a bailiff and his assistant looked like gaining entrance to a house. Kitchen has the phrase on his gravestone in West Norwood cemetery, south London.

Merryman. See BEST DOCTORS...; INS AND OUTS OF A...

mile. See LONGEST MILE IS...

Miles's boy told me. 'As a small child, many years ago, I used to be puzzled as to how my mother knew about all my dark deeds – when I'd told a fib; and she always knew where I'd been and who I'd been with *and* what I'd been up to. When I asked, she always replied this. How I grew to hate that boy!' – Anon (1998). Partridge/*Slang* has 'Miles's boy is spotted' as a printers' catchphrase, meaning 'We all know about *that*, addressed to anyone who, in a printing office, begins to spin a yarn: from *c.* 1830. Ex Miles, a Hampstead coach-boy celebrated for his faculty of diverting the passengers with anecdotes and tales.'

milk? [pronounced 'mil-uck' on a rising inflection]. Adopted in many households from Hermione Gingold (Drusilla), making tea for Alfred Marks (Edmond) in a feature called 'Mrs Doom's Diary' on the BBC radio show *Home at Eight* (first broadcast 21 April 1952). According to the *Independent* obituary of the show's scriptwriter Sid Colin (28 December 1989): 'Sid ingeniously combined Mrs Dale with Charles Addams in a series of sketches...[the Dooms] lived in a suburban castle with Fido, their pet alligator, and Trog, their giant speechless servant. At tea-time, people all over Britain were parroting the words that closed every Dooms sketch: "Tea, Edmond?" "Yes, thank you, dear – thank you." "Mil-uck?"'

When the sketches were included in another radio show, *Grande Gingold* (1955), the phrase became 'Tea, Gregory?... Milk?'

minds. See LITTLE THINGS PLEASE...

minor. See GO AND PARTAKE OF...

minute. See HAVEN'T I BEEN TELLING...

miserable. See SO MISERABLE THAT...

(a) moment on your lips, a lifetime on your hips. A dieter's slogan. Recorded in November 1987, but much older? 'Back in the 1960s/70s, my late mother-in-law had a more dietetically precise version: "A moment on the lips, a lifetime on the hips – that's chips"' – Michael Grosvenor Myer, Cambridgeshire (1999).

money. See HOW MUCH DOES IT...; THROWING HIS MONEY ABOUT...; WHICH WAS A LOT...

money is made round to go round. Proverb. 'When younger, I was questioned by my grandfather about a spending spree. In justification, I said, "Oh, Grandad, it's made round to go round." He replied, "Aye, lass, but it's made flat to pile up"' – Hylda M. Ball, Cheshire (1995).

Another version from Yorkshire: 'Money is made round to go round' – 'Nay, lad, it's made flat to stack.' Neither of these versions is much recorded in proverb books.

monkey. See AS THE MONKEY SAID...; DISAPPEARIO...; IT'S A MONKEY'S...

monkeys. See CRAFTY AS...; IN DAYS OF OLD...; PARROTS AND...

month. See NOT IN A MONTH OF...

more tea, Vicar? A correspondent who, understandably, wished to remain anonymous advanced this family phrase, 'for after a fart, or to cover any kind of embarrassment.' Paul Beale has collected various forms for a revision of Partridge/*Catch Phrases*, including: 'good evening, vicar!'; 'no swearing, please, vicar' (said facetiously to introduce a note of the mock-highbrow into a conversation full of expletives); 'another cucumber sandwich, vicar' (after an involuntary belch); 'speak up, Padre!/Brown/Ginger (you're through)' (as a response to a fart).

(the) more you cry – the less you'll pee. (Wickenden). 'When we used to cry as children, growing up in the Midlands, my mother would always say, "Stop yer blartin'" – to which my granny once replied, "Let 'em blart, they'll wee all the less"' – Martin Cheek, Broadstairs (1998). Partridge/*Catch Phrases* goes into this quite thoroughly: '"Let her cry: she'll piss the less"' was a semi-consolatory catch phrase...supposed to have been originally addressed as "the more you cry the less you'll piss", by sailors to their whores – or so Grose, 1796, tells us.'

Moses. See WHERE WAS MOSES WHEN...

mother. See DEAR MOTHER...; IT'S DARK/BLACK...; WHO'S SHE?...

mothers. See DON'T SOME...

(The) mountain sheep are sweeter,/But the valley sheep are fatter, / We therefore deemed it meeter/To carry off the latter. Proverb, though actually a quotation – from Thomas Love Peacock, *The Misfortunes of Elphin*, 'The War-Song of Dinas Vawr' (1829).

(like a stuffed) mourkin. 'When I was a lethargic teenager just hanging around doing nothing, my mother would admonish me by saying, "Don't just stand there like a stuffed mourkin"' – W.A. Vigs, Staffordshire (1996). 'Mourkin' is a Warwickshire word for a scarecrow, also spelt 'maukin'.

mouse. See MAY YOU NEVER MEET...; STRONG ENOUGH TO TROT...; WHY IS A...

mouth. See ALL MOUTH...; SHUT YOUR MOUTH...

muck. See YOU COULD GUESS...

musket. See LIKE A COW WITH...

must be hundreds of the buggers down there. 'My father-in-law was always dropping his back collar studs down the back of his neck. When he did, this is what he said' – Mrs O.L. Bennett, Berkshire (1995).

mustard on mutton is the sign of a glutton. Proverb. From my wife (1995). The nearest Apperson has to this is 'Mutton is meat for a glutton', dating from 1611.

mutton. See MUSTARD ON MUTTON...

(ee, mum,) my bum is numb. 'When sitting on a cold stone step, my father would say this' – Mrs Monica Nash, Nottinghamshire (1995).

my stomach thinks my throat's cut. 'I'm hungry' – as in Peter Nichols, *The Freeway*, Act 1, Scene 1 (1974). As 'My belly thinks my throat's cut', Apperson finds this in Palsgrave, *Acolastus* (1540).

N

nag. See WANTS TO KNOW THE INS AND OUTS...

name. See WHAT A NAME TO GO TO BED...

nature. See ANSWER THE CALL...

Nealopitan ice-cream. Mangled words. E. Jean Crossland, Nottinghamshire (1994). 'I've just recalled two variations on Neapolitan ice-cream: "Napoleon ice cream" and "Metropolitan ice cream"' – Mrs Monica Nash, Nottinghamshire (1995). But the most famous mangling of this name was probably originated by Frank Muir and Denis Norden in one of their 'The Glums' sketches from the BBC radio show *Take It From Here*. In the one where Ron first meets Eth (20 February 1957), we find this:

ETH: I like eating in the pictures, too.
RON: Do you? What's your favourite colour of the month?
ETH: Nealopitan.
RON: Ne – That's mine, too.
ETH: Is it?
RON: Yeah.
ETH: Well, isn't that strange? Oh – there's me, just

happening to find your cap, and then it turns out we both like Nealopitan ice-cream. Sends a shiver up your spine, doesn't it?

RON: If you have enough of it.

neat but not gaudy – like a bull's arse tied up with a bicycle chain. Told to me by an anonymous correspondent from the Cotswolds. Partridge/*Catch Phrases* suggests that the initial phrase 'neat but not gaudy' was established by about 1800, though in 1631 there had been the similar 'Comely, not gaudy'. Shakespeare in *Hamlet*, I.iii.71 (1600) has 'rich, not gaudy; / For the apparel oft proclaims the man...' The Revd Samuel Wesley wrote in 'An Epistle to a Friend concerning Poetry' (1700): 'Style is the dress of thought; a modest dress, / Neat, but not gaudy, will true critics please.' Charles Lamb wrote to William Wordsworth (June 1806), 'A little thin flowery border round, neat not gaudy.' John Ruskin, writing in the *Architectural Magazine* (November 1838): 'That admiration of the "neat but gaudy" which is commonly reported to have influenced the devil when he painted his tail pea green.' Indeed, Partridge cites: 'Neat, but not gaudy, as the monkey said, when he painted his tail sky blue' and '...painted his bottom pink and tied up his tail with pea-green.' See also AS THE MONKEY SAID...; SKY BLUE PINK...

needle. See SHIT THROUGH THE EYE OF...

neither arse nor elbow. 'Anything doubtful' – aunt of Doris Humphrey, Lincolnshire (1995). Note also that 'my elbow!' is a euphemistic version of the exclamation 'my arse!'

neither shape nor make to it. 'Clothes criticism' – Stella Richardson, Essex (1998).

Nelson. See WHEN NELSON GETS HIS EYE...

never buy a saddle until you meet the horse. 'A saying of my late grandfather' – John O'Byrne, Dublin (1998).

never chase girls or buses – there will (always) be another one coming along soon. Partridge/*Catch Phrases* dates this from the 1920s and derives it from the early US version with 'streetcars' instead of 'buses'. Compare the allusion to the saying by Derick Heathcoat Amory when British Chancellor of the Exchequer (1958–60): 'There are three things not worth running for – a bus, a woman or a new economic panacea; if you wait a bit another one will come along.'

never discuss a disaster – 'twill bring another one faster. Informal proverb. Quoted in Mary Killen, *Best Behaviour* (1990).

(he) never likes to get up before the streets are aired. 'On a late riser' – said by the mother of Richard Knowles, London SW12 (1998) about him.

(oh well,) never mind, you're a long time dead. Consolatory phrase. 'Whenever my mother is regaled with a tale of disastrous experience, or a chain of calamitous events, she always makes this comment' – Nellie Jarvis, Nottinghamshire (2000). This appears in 'Number Two' of John Osborne's play *The Entertainer* (1957). Partridge/ *Catch Phrases* has it as a variation of (the mostly 20th century) 'You'll be a long time dead.'

never say die while you've a chop in the locker. 'A friend's father used to say this' – E. Jean Crossland,

Nottinghamshire (1994). The basic expression, 'never say die!', meaning 'never give in', was much used by Charles Dickens in his writings, starting with 'Greenwich Fair' in *Sketches by Boz* (written 1833–6) – though it is presumably not original to him. It occurs in *The Pickwick Papers* (1836–7) and is notably the catchphrase of Grip, the raven, in Barnaby Rudge (1841). W. Gurney Benham, *Cassell's Book of Quotations* (1907) has, 'Never say die./Up, man, and try!' in the proverbs section, but undated.

never show a fool half-finished work. Proverb. 'My father said, "Never show a fool half-finished work" – always used as a retort to someone who came along and offered comment (or worse still criticism) while you were grappling with a job like cooking, sewing or DIY' – Robert Craig, London N12 (1996).

never trouble trouble till trouble troubles you. Nannyism (Casson/Grenfell). There was a song 'Trouble', written by David Keppel and was known by 1916:

> Never trouble trouble
> Till trouble troubles you
> For if you trouble trouble
> You'll only double trouble
> And trouble others too.

Apperson has the first two lines recorded as a proverbial saying, in Derby, from the *Folk-Lore Journal* (1884).

never wrestle with a chimney sweep. Don't resort to dirty tricks. From the *Observer* Magazine (4 July 1993) on Tony Benn MP: 'Now he is older he finds himself repeating advice his father offered him as a child like "never wrestle with a chimney sweep", which means don't soil yourself by responding to your opponents' dirty tricks. "The whole wisdom of humanity is summed up in these phrases," he muses.' Benn had earlier used the phrase in connection with the Profumo affair in 1963. From Ben Pimlott, *Harold Wilson* (1992): 'For the Labour Party to rub its hands with glee, as Wedgwood Benn put it, would be like wrestling with a chimney sweep.'

Compare a conversation between Dr Johnson and Dr William Adams in Boswell's *Life of Johnson* (for 20 March 1776): 'JOHNSON: If my antagonist writes bad language, though that may not be essential to the question, I will attack him for his bad language. ADAMS: You would not jostle a chimney-sweeper. JOHNSON: Yes, Sir, if it were necessary to jostle him *down*.'

Newgate. See AS BLACK...

nibble. See EVERY TIME...

(the) nicest things come in smallest parcels. Nannyism (Casson/Grenfell). A version of 'the best things come in small packages', a proverb well established by the late 19th century (*CODP*).

Nick. See LIKE THE COLOUR OF OLD...

night. See HEAVEN HELP...

Night-night, sleep tight/Mind that the fleas don't bite. Nursery valediction. Or 'good night... mind the fleas and bugs don't bite.' 'I was told on a visit to the American Museum in Bath that early settlers in America built traditional wooden bed frames and then "strung" them, rather like tennis racquets. The most comfortable sleep was deemed to be likely on a bed that had been *tightly* strung. Presumably if a bed were slack, then the occupant might well drop to the floor through the meshing!' – Brian Adams, Berkshire (1997). Casson/Grenfell has: 'Goodnight, sleep tight, mind the fleas don't bite. If they do, get a shoe and crack their little heads in two.'

no. See DON'T SAY 'NO'...

'No answer' was the stern reply! An ironic comment on the fact that no one has replied or said a word. Known by the 1930s but in various forms, including: '"No answer, no answer" came the loud reply' and '"Shrieks of silence" was the stern reply'. If these are quotations, the original source has not been identified. Compare, however, 'But answer came there none – /And this was scarcely odd, because/ They'd eaten every one' – Lewis Carroll, *Through the Looking Glass* (1872), 'The Walrus and the Carpenter' episode. 'But answer came there none' is a phrase that also appears in Scott (*The Bridal of Triermain*, 1813) and almost in Shakespeare ('But answer made it none', *Hamlet*, I.ii.215). It has also been suggested that the phrase might have been a joke response to the opening question in Walter de la Mare's poem 'The Listeners' (1912): '"Is there anybody there?" said the Traveller,/Knocking on the moonlit door.' The actual answer in the poem is '"Tell them I came, and no one answered,/ That I kept my word," he said.'

'My mother (1896–1968) used to say "No answer was the stern reply," especially if her children didn't answer her questions. Now I, my husband and my son often use the phrase – especially if there's no reply when we phone each other! I have tried to trace its origins with no success, though I have a feeling it may come from a monologue' – Mrs M. White, Surrey (1994). Among variations: 'No answer, no answer came the loud reply' – an Edinburgh grandmother, 1960s, of the Revd Lorna Rattray (1994); 'Silence was the stern reply' – Paul Beale (1994); '"No answer was the stern reply,/ The old fishmonger has gone by" – this was current in my 1920s childhood in North Lancashire, said lugubriously. Either a monologue (Billy Bennett?) or an earlier hammy melodrama as source' – N.P. Griffin, Lancashire (1997); 'My father used to complete this as a non-rhyming couplet: "No answer came the stern reply/As he got on his bike and walked away!"' – Dick Frazer, Norfolk (1997).

no good getting old if you don't get crafty. 'Old people's outlook, on some others' (Wickenden).

no good poking the fire when the ashes have gone cold. 'On love gone cold' (Wickenden).

no more sense than they were born with. 'Of daft people' (Wickenden).

no one ever died of a bad smell. Informal proverb, told to me by Katharine Whitehorn (1992).

noise. See MAKE A NOISE...

North. See GO NORTH.

nose. See LOOK OVER YOUR HEADS...; POWDER ONE'S NOSE ; STOP PICKING YOUR...; YOU'D LAUGH TO SEE YOUR MOTHER'S...; YOUR NOSE SMELLS...; YOUR NOSE WILL...

noses. See FIGHTING ONE MINUTE...

not a word about the pig and how it died, and whose small potatoes it ate. 'My grandmother (92) has this saying – I'd love to know where it comes from' – Kate Pool, London SW10 (1995). The only clue I have found is a headline in *Punch* (20 August 1864) – 'Not a Word About the Pig'. Partridge/*Slang* has 'Not a word of the pudding' = 'say nothing about the matter', dated late 17th century.

not in a month of Sundays. 'About a task that would never be accomplished' – Stella Richardson, Essex (1998). *OED2* has the phrase 'month of Sundays' = 'long time' in a Captain Marryat novel, *Newton Forster* (1832).

not so green as cabbage-looking. Not such a fool [or as innocent] as may appear. 'If you explained things in too much detail or she thought you were talking down to her, my aunt would say: "I'm not so green as I'm cabbage looking" [i.e. I'm not green, just cabbage looking]' – Mrs J. Payne, North Yorkshire (1995). 'My Grandma, who lived almost all her life in the West Riding of Yorkshire, had a different version when anyone, usually me, tried to beat her at something with a trick. It was, "I'm not as daft as I'm cabbage looking"' – Norman Woollons, East Yorkshire (2000). '"I may be cabbage-looking but I'm not green" – better sense?' – Stella Richardson, Essex (1998).

This expression appears to have been around since the late 19th century. How about this from James Joyce, *Ulysses* (1922): 'Gob, he's not as green as he's cabbagelooking'?

nourishment. See IT'S NOURISHMENT...

(there's) nowt so queer as folks. There's nothing so odd as people. 'And not really my mother's – it is still used today all over the North of England – "There's nowt so queer as folks – 'cept folks's childer"' – Margaret Rowden, Somerset (1995). Partridge/*Catch Phrases* dates this from the second half of the 19th century.

nutting bag. See LIKE THE COLOUR OF OLD ...

O

o'clock. See DON'T STAND . . . ; HEAVENS, ELEVEN . . .

oats. See UGLY ENOUGH TO EAT OATS.

off we go and the colour's pink. In 1980, Anthony Smith of Pinner, Middlesex queried the origin of this phrase which he said was used when restarting some social activity/topic of conversation/fresh round of drinks. Many years later, Donald Hickling of Northampton commented: 'I heard this catchphrase in 'Metroland' (to the north of Pinner and slightly to the left) in a respectable hostelry one Saturday lunchtime when the host or master of ceremonies, a WW2 naval officer, was remembering how a liberal supply of pink gins kept him going, and he assumed that everyone in his company appreciated "pinkers". And, in the context of family sayings, I can quote the parent of a friend who was wont to exclaim, "Up she goes and her knickers are pink". Metroland again!'

off-stump. See GO TO THE OFF-STUMP

Oh King, live forever! A Mr Howells introduced Mark Twain at a seventieth birthday dinner at Delmonico's restaurant, New York City (5 December 1905), with these words: 'I will try not to be greedy on your behalf in wishing the health of our honored and, in view of his great age, our revered guest. I will not say, "Oh King, live forever!" but "Oh King, live as long as you like!"'

It has been a traditional toast or wish that kings live for ever or, at the very least, a long time. The Japanese cry '*Banzai*', directed at the Emperor, literally means no more than 'ten thousand years', but its more usual meaning is 'for a long time'. In full, '*Tenno heika banzai*' – 'Long live the Emperor', is a phrase that goes back into Japanese history, despite its appropriation by the nationalist movements of the 1930s. The phrase is still in use. If literally translated, it is really no different from: 'Zadok the priest, and Nathan the prophet, anointed Solomon king. And all the people rejoiced and said, God save the king. Long live the king, *may the king live for ever*. Amen. Alleluia' – which has been sung at the coronation of almost every English sovereign since William of Normandy was crowned in Westminster Abbey on Christmas Day 1066.

Jonathan Swift includes 'may you live a thousand years' among the conversational chestnuts in *Polite Conversation* (1738). The Sergeant in Charles Dickens, *Great Expectations*, Chap. 5 (1860–1) incorporates it in a toast. Compare TRUE, O KING!

Oh look, Mama, what have we here that looks like strawberry jam?/Hush, hush, my dear 'tis your papa – run over by a tram! 'When using ham we always say this rhyme. Also, when we see cakes in a baker's window, we say, "Struck through the heart like a penny treacle tart". Friends, I am sure, think we are mad, but it's like a private joke to us and it's good to think that my grandparents are still alive in word if not in person' – Gail Cromack, Carmarthenshire

(1998). Linda Addison, Northamptonshire (1999), sent the slightly different: 'Oh, mother dear/What is this here/That looks like raspberry jam/Hush, hush my dear/It's poor papa/Run over by a tram.'

old. See IN DAYS OF OLD...; NO GOOD GETTING OLD...

older. See LITTLE OLDER THAN MY TEETH...

once every Preston Guild. 'Of a rare occurrence' – Stella Richardson, Essex (1998). Partridge/*Slang* has this as a Lancashire colloquialism. Preston Guild (or Gild) is/was held only every twenty years.

one o' them as is either up on the roof or down the well. 'Of a temperamental person' – Flora Thompson, *Lark Rise*, Chap. 3 (1939).

orange. See SO MEAN HE CAN PEEL...

orchid. See GO AND SHAKE THE...

out. See BETTER OUT...; THERE'S MORE OUT THAN IN.

oven. See LIKE A PARISH OVEN.

P

P.M.K. (Plenty More in Kitchen). Initial code. M.S. Peebles, City of Glasgow (1999).

page. See GO TO PAGE 54.

pair. See THERE'S A PAIR OF YOU THERE...; THEY'D SPOIL ANOTHER PAIR.

palaces. See IF IT WAS RAINING...

pantry. See TWO JUMPS AT THE PANTRY DOOR...

parcels. See NICEST THINGS COME...

pardon. See 'WHAT?'S DEAD LONG AGO...

(oops,) pardon, Mrs Arden, there's a pig in your garden! What you exclaim after belching or burping, in order to deflect attention from yourself. In 1997, the *Sunday Telegraph* Magazine started a picture puzzle series under the title 'Pardon, Mrs Arden' and I was asked where the phrase came from. I had never heard it, but diligent research unearthed these citations: from the *Daily Mail* (19

March 1994); 'It was blissful to lie in my adjoining single bed, watching her undress down to her vest and pink satin bloomers, averting my gaze while she used what she called the "Edgar Allan", then listening to the crunch of biscuits, the slurp of gin and tonic and the occasional gentle belch, followed by an apologetic murmur of "Oops! Pardon Mrs Arden!"'; and from the *Daily Telegraph* (29 January 1994); 'Every time you said "pardon" to old Charlie, who worked on the farm, he would answer: "Pardon, Mrs Arden, there's a pig in your garden".'

At this point, my wife woke up and added (from her Buckinghamshire childhood) the variant: '... there's a *pig* in your *back* garden', plus the rejoinder, 'That bain't no pig, that be my son, John.' Curiouser and curiouser. Latterly, it has been suggested to me that there was a novelty song with the title 'Pardon, Mrs Arden', continuing, 'There's a kitten in your garden/Saying miaow, miaow, miaow, miaow/Isn't it a pity that it's such a pretty kitty/Saying miaow etc.' I have been unable to trace this. However, it does seem to be the case that there was an 1870s music hall song beginning, 'Beg your parding, Mrs Harding,/Is my kitting in your garding?' It is referred to in Vyvyan Holland's book *Son of Oscar Wilde* (1954):

> Parding Mrs Harding,
> Is our kitting in your garding,
> Eating of a mutting-bone?
> No, he's gone to Londing.
> How many miles to Londing?
> Eleving? I thought it was only seving.
> Heavings! *What* a long way from home!

This couplet may also have been included:

I'm sorry, Missus Dewsberry
I haven't seen her since last Tuesberry.

H. Montgomery Hyde's *Oscar Wilde* (1976) has the first two lines as, rather: 'Beg your parding, Mrs Harding,/Is my kitting in your garding?'; and Kathleen Strange remembered the first three lines (1997, when she was 92) as 'I beg your parding, Mrs 'Arding/Is my kitting in your garding/Eating of a herring-bone?' It is not hard to see how the expression 'pardon, Mrs Arden' could have developed from this.

Paris. See GO TO PARIS ; IT'S SNOWING...

parish. See LIKE A PARISH OVEN.

parrots and monkeys. Goods and chattels, personal possessions. 'Whenever we were about to embark on a trip my father used to say, "Pick up your monkeys and parrots, fall in facing the boat and don't knock the blooming thing over" – he claims it was common parlance in the Third Hussars but I've never met another Third Hussar to prove it!' – John Brooks, Gloucestershire (1998). Partridge/*Slang* has this as *Navy* slang since about 1930 and derives it from the returning seaman's pets and souvenirs.

parsnips. See FINE WORDS...

parson. See IT'S ENOUGH TO MAKE...

parts. See DON'T PUT YOUR...

path. See UP/DOWN THE GARDEN PATH.

patience and perseverance... 'I live in the West Midlands. A few miles from here at Rowley Regis are quarries where they blast a very hard local rock known as Rowley Rag. My Gran used to say that: "Patience and perseverance will saw through Rowley Rag with a feather"' – Patricia M. Rodwell, West Midlands (1995). Compare this with the rhyme recalled by Jim Snell of West Sussex (1998), as said to him in his childhood (around 1918) by his mother: 'Patience and perseverance/Made a bishop of His Reverence.'

patience is a virtue, virtue is a grace/Grace was a little girl who wouldn't wash her face. 'If anyone mentioned patience, or the lack of it, one of my aunts used to say this' – Sylvia Dowling, Lancashire (1998). 'Patience is a virtue' was a proverb by the 15th century. Casson/Grenfell has, rather: 'Patience is a virtue, virtue is a grace./Put them both together, and you get a pretty face.'

pea. See TO HELL WITH...

peach. See GO AND SQUEEZE...; PEEL A PEACH FOR...

pearls before swine. See AGE BEFORE BEAUTY.

(they're getting) peas above sticks. 'On people bettering themselves' – Stella Richardson, Essex (1998). 'I had an aunt who had an apt and witty saying for every eventuality – sometimes rather sharp and not very kind, but always apt. Of anyone she knew who had got above themselves, she would say, "The peas have grown above the sticks"' – Doris Humphrey, Grantham (1995).

peck. See YOU HAVE TO EAT A PECK...

pee. See GO AND SEE THE TURK...; PLAY WITH FIRE...

peel. See SO MEAN HE CAN PEEL...

peel a peach for one's enemy, peel a pear for a friend. Proverb. 'One peels a peach for one's enemy because there is something in the skin which counteracts the harmful acid which is round the pip. One peels a pear for a friend for a similar reason – i.e. the harmful acid is just below the skin of that fruit' – Mrs Ann Turner, East Sussex (1995).

pennies. See STEAL THE PENNIES OFF...

penny. See PUT A PENNY ON...; SPEND A PENNY WITHOUT...

(a) penny bun costs twopence when you have a woman with you. 'This was my father-in-law's advice to my husband when we started courting' – Mrs Rita M. Kirton, West Yorkshire (1995).

Percy. See POINT PERCY AT...

Percy Topliss. See YOU'RE AS DAFT...

perfection is only to be found in the dictionary. Informal proverb – 'a favourite of my grandmother who died in 1955' – Joan Whitworth, Cumbria (1995). Compare 'The only place where success comes before work is in a dictionary' – the hairdresser Vidal Sassoon quoting a teacher in 1980.

perseverance. See PATIENCE AND...

phrase. See GOING THROUGH A...

pick. See IT'LL NEVER GET WELL...

picnic. See COUPLE OF...

picture-skew. Mangled words. 'My father, a proficient reader and speller, purposely mispronounced "picturesque" as "picture-skew" and "marmalade" as "marmal-a-dee"' – Mrs K.A. King, Gloucestershire (1995).

piddled. See EVERY LITTLE...

pieces. See SAVE THE PIECES...

Piff(e)y. See SIT LIKE PIFF(E)Y.

pig. See AS AWKWARD...; DEAR MOTHER...; GO TO PUTNEY...; NOT A WORD ABOUT THE PIG...; PARDON, MRS ARDEN...; WHAT DO YOU EXPECT FROM A PIG...; YUM, YUM...

pig-shit. See IGNORANT AS...

pink. See OFF WE GO AND...; SKY BLUE PINK...

pitchers. See LITTLE PITCHERS HAVE...

(a) place for everything and everything in its place. A prescription for orderly domestic arrangements. The writer Charles Osborne (who grew up in Australia) remembered being an untidy child and his mother's nannyish admonition (and quite a well-known saying it is, too). Samuel Smiles quotes it in *Thrift* (1875) but he had been preceded by the illustrious Mrs (Isabella) Beeton in *The Book of Household Management*, Chap. 2 (1861). One feels that Mrs Beeton was probably more interested in domestic order than in making delicious food. The saying was not original to her, however, as is plain from the following earlier uses. George Herbert had the basic idea in his *Outlandish Proverbs* (1640): 'All things have their place, knew we how to place them.' Captain Marryat in *Masterman Ready*, Bk 2, Chap. 1 (1842) has: 'In a well-conducted man-of-war...everything in its place, and there is a place for every thing.' Then there is this Wellerism from *Yankee Blade* (18 May 1848): '"A place for everything and everything in its place", as an old lady said when she stowed the broom, bellows, balls of yarn, cards, caps, curry-comb, three cats and a gridiron into an old oven.'

play with fire, pee in the bed. A taunt to a child. My wife remembers it from Buckinghamshire in the 1950s and still finds it inexplicable.

pleasant dreams, sweet repose: all the bed and all the clothes. 'A goodnight wish' – mother of Marjorie Wild, Devon (2000).

plumbing. See GO AND CHECK THE PLUMBING.

plus fours and no breakfast. 'My aunts tell me that this was a remark always attributed to the nouveau riche, who wore all they had on their backs. Everything for show and no stability' – Mrs D.E. Thorn, Lincolnshire (1998). 'Speaks rather fancy; truculent; plausible; a bit of a shower-off; plus-fours and no breakfast, you know...a gabbing, ambitious, mock-tough, pretentious young man' – Dylan Thomas characterising himself in a broadcast, 'Return Journey' (1947). I suppose the implication is that the 'shower-off' is someone of limited means who spends what he has on flashy clothes and therefore can't afford any breakfast.

Then the variations: '"Plus fours and kippers for breakfast" had to do with genteel poverty in upper class Jesmond' – from an 89-year-old in Newcastle upon Tyne (1998). 'Fur coats and no breakfast' – Stella Richardson, Essex (1998). '"All crepe sole and bay windows", said in an exaggerated posh voice (with an "h" in "whindows")' – Dave Hopkins, Kent (1998). Paul Beale commented: '"Plus fours and no breakfast" seems to equate to "(all) bay-windows and no breakfast" = sacrificing everything for the sake of an appearance of social superiority. I heard "bay windows" soon after we came to live in Leicestershire 25 years ago.' Beale also rounded up: 'kippers and curtains', 'brown boots and no breakfast', 'empty bellies and brass doorknobs'. See also ALL CURTAINS...; ALL FUR COAT...

po. See HEAVENS, ELEVEN...

pockets. See THERE ARE NO...

(to) point Percy at the porcelain. Loophemism. An Australianism (not of his own invention) introduced to Britain by Barry Humphries through the 'Barry Mackenzie' strip in *Private Eye* (1960s/70s).

polish. See COULD I POLISH...

Pomme. See GO TO LA POMME...

porridge. See SAVE YOUR BREATH TO...

potatoes. See COULD GROW...

potatoes and point. Fobbing-off phrase. 'My Cumbrian

grandmother would say this when asked what was for lunch...' – Janet C. Egan, Middlesex (2000).

poultice. See PUTTING A POULTICE ON...

poverty. See TO HELL WITH...; WHEN POVERTY COMES IN...

poverty's no disgrace but it's a damn nuisance. 'My mother – born and bred a Lancastrian, but all Welsh forbears, was a great one for sayings. Although I've heard many variations of one of her remarks, I first heard this aphorism in my own home' – Miss L. Williams, Greater Manchester (1993). Compare 'Poverty of course is no disgrace, but it is damned annoying' – attributed to William Pitt, British Prime Minister (1759–1806) in *The Treasury of Humorous Quotations*, ed. Evan Esar & Nicolas Bentley (1951). As 'Poverty's no disgrace, but 'tis a great inconvenience', this was said to be 'a common saying among the *Lark Rise* people' in Flora Thompson, *Lark Rise*, Chap. 1 (1939). Apperson finds it in John Florio, *Second Frutes* (1591), in the form: 'Poverty is no vice but an inconvenience'.

(to) powder one's nose. Loophemism – female use only. Partridge/*Slang* dates this from 1940 onwards.

praise. See APPROBATION FROM...

prayers. See SAYS ANYTHING BUT HIS...

press. See CAN I PRESS...

Preston Guild. See ONCE EVERY...

price. See CHEAP AT HALF...; WHAT'S THAT GOT TO DO WITH...

promise. See LICK AND A PROMISE.

(the) proof of the pudding is in the lap of the gods. The father of the philosopher Bryan Magee used to say this (as he recalled on BBC Radio *Quote...Unquote,* 18 December 1990): 'I think it was a line from a play he'd seen with Mrs Patrick Campbell. We always used to say it when anything was uncertain.'

pudding. See PROOF OF THE PUDDING...; WAIT-AND-SEE PUDDING

(you'd laugh to see a) pudding crawl. 'My mother-in-law would say this to children who were having a fit of the giggles for no reason' – Mira Little, Somerset (1999). 'Said when someone laughs at something silly or for no apparent reason' – by the grandmother of the wife of Arthur Haseler, London N22 (2000). Compare 'What would shock me would make a pudding crawl' – it would take an awful lot to shock me (a female), by 1900, according to Partridge/*Catch Phrases.*

puddings. See PUT ONE'S PUDDINGS OUT...; TOO SLOW TO CARRY...

pullet/pullit. See BREAD AND PULLET...

pump. See GO AND PUMP...

pump-handles. See KNOBS AND CHAIRS...

pump-water. See FACE LIKE A YARD...

punch. See COULDN'T PUNCH...

Punch has done dancing. 'When I was a child, some 45 years ago, my father had a favourite saying. This was said to us children when he had had enough of playing with us or when it was time to finish anything we were doing, including fighting' – Colin Platt, Kent (1998). Partridge/*Catch Phrases* has this as referring to the Punch of Punch-and-Judy puppetry and general folklore, dating from the second half of the 19th century, and meaning 'I can no longer dance to your tune – a tune of requests and solicitations.'

punishment. See IT'S NOURISHMENT...

pussy. See DOESN'T KNOW PUSSY...; LIKE WHEN PUSSY BURNS...

put a half on top of this one. 'My father would never drink all of his cup of tea. If he was asked if he would like a fresh cup, he would say, "Just put a half on top of this one"' – Mrs K.Y. Williams, Herefordshire (1998).

put a penny on the drum. A phrase spoken by a comedian called Clay Keyes in a BBC radio show called *The Old Town Hall* in the early 1940s. But several *Quote...Unquote* listeners wrote to say that the phrase definitely existed before then. For example, Stanley Holloway recorded a song with the title 'Penny on the Drum' in 1937, beginning 'Will you please put a penny on the drum...' And Jean Phillips of Henley-on-Thames wrote: 'According to my father, who was in the army in the First World War, it was an invitation to take part in Crown and Anchor, a gambling game, requiring a board and some dice, marked with Crown and Anchor. The person starting the game would call out, "Put a penny on the drum", and anyone who did so could then take part in the game. I think the use of an actual drum had been superseded and the game may well have been played on the ground.' Jim Bennet of Halifax, Nova Scotia, meanwhile remembered 'an irreverent song about the Salvation Army chiefly sung by rude adolescent boys in the 1940s: "Halleluiah, halleluiah, throw a nickel on the drum and you'll be saved" – obviously a reference to the Army's street-corner band concerts, where the drum would be set up as a depository for coins from passers-by.'

(to) put one's puddings out for treacle. In May 1994, Teresa Gorman MP accused Michael Heseltine of disloyalty to Prime Minister John Major by saying that he was 'putting his puddings out for treacle.' Mrs Gorman subsequently explained her expression to Alan Watkins in the *Independent on Sunday* (12 June 1994): '[It] was used in our neighbourhood about any woman considered to be putting herself forward for attention – or suspected of paying the tradesmen's bills in "kind"!'

'I recall hearing this on a 1935–45 wartime radio comedy programme. A character in a "soppy" voice said, "They told us to put our puddings out for treacle. I put mine out, and somebody pinched me pudding!"' – John Smart, Essex (2000). Indeed: 'Somebody pinched me puddin'!' was used by the variety act Collinson and Breen. Their explanation was that, 'Somebody said "All put your puddins out for treacle", and I put mine out and somebody pinched it!'

Partridge/*Catch Phrases* has, rather, 'put your pudden up for treacle!' as 'encouragement to be forthcoming' and quotes Edgar T. Brown (1977): 'I met the phrase in the Army in 1914 and my informant told me that it relates to prison. If you were unwise enough to "old your pudden out for treacle" it would have been swiped by another inmate, who "knew the ropes" better than you did.'

Putney. See GO TO PUTNEY...

(like) putting a poultice on a wooden leg. 'When trying to persuade or encourage someone who did not respond' – Flora Thompson, *Lark Rise*, Chap. 3 (1939).

putting an equal strain on all parts. I.e. going to bed – T. Braun, London SW3 (1996).

QR

queer. See AS QUEER AS...; NOWT SO QUEER AS...

quiet. See ANYTHING FOR A QUIET...; BEST DOCTORS...

rabbit. See HOPE YOUR...; IF A RABBIT RAN...; LET THE DOG SEE...; LIKE A FERRET...

racing. See LICKS HEN RACING.

radiator. See GO AND DRAIN...

rain. See IT'LL EITHER RAIN...

(to) rain cats and dogs. Meaning 'to rain extremely heavily'. Known by 1738 (Swift, *Polite Conversation*), though there is a 1652 citation: 'Raining dogs and polecats'. Shelley wrote 'raining cats and dogs' in a letter to a friend (1819). There is no very convincing explanation for this phrase. According to the *Morris Dictionary of Word and Phrase Origins* (1977), it comes from the days when street drainage was so poor that a heavy rain storm could easily drown cats and dogs. After the storm people would see the number of dead cats and dogs and think it looked as if they had fallen out of the sky. *Brewer's Dictionary of Phrase and Fable* (1989) suggests, on the other hand, that in northern mythology cats were supposed to have great influence on the weather and dogs were a signal of wind, 'thus cat may be taken as a symbol of the downpouring rain, and the dog of the strong gusts of wind accompanying a rain-storm.'

raining. See IF IT WAS RAINING...

rare. See MANNERS AMONG TANNERS...

(every) rat smells its own hole. 'If someone tried to blame a bad smell on someone else' (Wickenden).

red hat. See ALL FUR COAT...

remember Belgium! 'My mother used to say this to me in the 1930s when, as a small boy, I showed signs of being about to do something she disapproved of. The meaning was clear – "remember what happened to *them*" – presumably in 1914' – Guy Braithwaite, Middlesex (1998). Indeed, 'Remember Belgium!' was an actual recruiting slogan referring to the invasion of Belgium by the Germans at the start of the First World War. It eventually emerged with ironic emphasis amid the mud of Ypres, encouraging the rejoinder: 'As if I'm ever likely to forget the bloody place!' (Partridge/*Catch Phrases*).

rest. See AND THE REST.

return. See IF I RETURN...

rice pudding. See COULDN'T KNOCK.

(you could) ride to York on that lip. 'To a sulking person' – Stella Richardson, Essex (1998). Because the drooping lip looked like a saddle? Casson/Grenfell has the nannyism: 'I could ride to London on that lip.'

ring. See GO AND WRING...

rock-of-eye. See DO BY...

roof. See ONE O' THEM AS IS EITHER...

rooks. See WONDER TILL THE ROOKS...

room. See GO TO THE SMALLEST...; UP IN ANNIE'S ROOM...

roper. See DOG BITE OLD...

roses. See IF THEY FELL DOWN...

rudest. See WHAT ARE THE THREE...

rule of thumb. See DO BY...

running in and out like a blue-arsed fly. 'Of someone hurrying' (Wickenden).

(it) runs in the family like wooden legs. 'My wife had an unusual expression, which she would use when we might be discussing peculiarities of a certain family, such as the way they all walk in the same manner, or talk in a similar way. She would say, "It runs in the family like wooden legs"' – Neil G. Clark, South Yorkshire (1996). Apperson finds this in Bridge, *Cheshire Proverbs* (1917): '*It* *runs in the blood like wooden legs.* I heard this saying from the mouth of an Ulsterman, in Surrey, in the sixties of the last century.'

rush. See DON'T RUSH SO . . .

S

sacked for eating the soap. 'This was a saying of my late mother and I assume it originated in Dublin, her birthplace, although I never heard anyone else use it. It is a response to that dreadful habit of name-dropping: "Ah, yes...his mother used to wash for us but we sacked her for eating the soap"' – Paul Dann, Surrey (1995). Compare: 'To put down the arrogant: "Well, he used to chew bread for our ducks but one day I caught him swallowing some so we gave him the sack!"' – Lorna Hanks, Hampshire (1995). 'My father hated name-dropping and if some pompous person started some lengthy anecdote during which he/she namedropped with gusto, he would interrupt with: "Ah, yes! He/she used to cut chaff for our ducks." It was a guaranteed conversation stopper' – Diana Negus, Leicestershire (1996).

saddle. See NEVER BUY A...

sailor. See ENOUGH BLUE...

sailors. See HEAVEN HELP...

St Paul's. See GIVE SOMEONE THE...

same thing, different gravy. 'When comparing dishes in a restaurant, my father always used to make this complaint' – Dave Hopkins, Kent (1998).

(and the) same to you with (brass) knobs on! 'With knobs on' simply means 'generous, embellished'. Partridge/ *Slang* suggests that this was known by 1910. In 1987, Margaret Walsh of Auckland, New Zealand, told me of this baroque version: 'Same to you with brass fittings and a self-starter'.

sandwiches. See COUPLE OF...

sausage. See GOD BREEZE ME...; SILENCE IS GOLDEN...

(The) sausage was a fat one/The outside was a skin./The Inside was the mystery/Of a dog called Little Jim. 'My mother's quip when we had sausages for dinner' – Mrs H. Acklin, Essex (1998).

save the pieces – Mother likes the pattern. 'Said when anything is heard to drop or be broken' – Bob Hart, Powys (2000).

save your breath to cool your porridge. I.e. stop talking at table. A nannyism in Casson/Grenfell. A proverb in similar form existed by the late 16th century (*ODP*).

(he/she) says anything but his/her prayers. Apperson finds 'He says anything but his prayers and then he whistles' in 1732; six years later, Swift has this in *Polite Conversation*: 'Miss will say any Thing but her Prayers, and those she whistles'.

scissor. See AS MUCH USE...

sea. See EVERY LITTLE...; WORSE THINGS HAPPEN AT...

see. See I SEE...; BLIND MAN...

(to) see how the cat jumps. 'As a child of the 1930s, money was very scarce. Whenever I asked my mother for something – sweets, clothes, bus ride, shoes, etc. – her answer was always the same: "I shall have to see how the cat jumps". Needless to say, I was always watching the cat' – Mrs I.N. Knight, Surrey (1998). Partridge/*Slang* defines this as 'watching the course of events before committing oneself to decision or action' and dates it from about 1820. Apperson finds it in Sir Walter Scott's *Journal* (7 October 1826).

semi-skilled milk. Mangled words – E. Jean Crossland, Nottinghamshire (1994).

sense. See IT WON'T HURT...; NO MORE SENSE THAN...

servant. See WHAT DID YOUR LAST SERVANT...

sewer. See IF THEY FELL DOWN...

sewing. See EVERYTHING A LADY...

sewn with a hot needle and a burnt thread. 'Clothes criticism' – Stella Richardson, Essex (1998).

shake. See GO AND SHAKE...

shake yourself and give the hens a feed. I.e. get a move on. 'From my Dad' – Anon.

shape. See NEITHER SHAPE NOR ...

sharp. See BACK IN THE KNIFE-BOX ...

shed. See GO AND SHED ...

sheep. See EVERY TIME ...; MOUNTAIN SHEEP ARE ...

Sheerness. See CHEER UP FOR ...

shepherd before sheep! See AGE BEFORE BEAUTY.

shilling. See COUPLE OF ...; LOOK LIKE YOU'VE LOST ...

(there –) shining like shit on a barn door! 'My mother's *pièce de resistance* was saved for the polishing of furniture or cleaning windows. She would stand back and with a sigh of satisfaction exclaim this' – Margaret Martin, Surrey (1993). Partridge/*Slang* has 'shine like a shitten barn door' and finds an allusion to the phrase in Swift's *Polite Conversation* (1738): 'Why, Miss, you shine this Morning like a sh-- Barn-Door'.

shit. See DOESN'T KNOW WHETHER ...; SHINING LIKE SHIT ON ...; THINKS HIS/HER SHIT ...; WISH IN ONE HAND ...

shit before the shovel. See AGE BEFORE BEAUTY.

(to) shit through the eye of a needle. 'On taking syrup of figs for constipation: "Take this and you'll s--t through the eye of a needle"' (Wickenden). Partridge/*Catch Phrases* has 'I could shit through the eye of a needle' and 'without touching the sides', to describe this unpleasant condition however caused (and not just by a hangover).

shoes. See HE CAN LEAVE...

shone. See IT SHONE LIKE A...

(that was) short and sweet like a jackass's gallop. 'On something very short' (Wickenden). Apperson has 'short and sweet like a donkey's gallop' (from *Lancs Sayings*, 1901), which makes rather more sense. Perhaps 'jackass's' is from 'ass's' out of 'donkey's'? I am irresistibly reminded of the Revd Sydney Smith's remark (1809) about an article submitted to the *Edinburgh Review* by Lord Macaulay, that it was 'long yet vigorous, like the penis of a jackass'. No connection, surely?

(don't) shout before you get hurt. 'If someone thought they would get blamed unnecessarily' (Wickenden).

shouting. See ALL THE SHOUTING...

shrouds. See THERE ARE NO POCKETS IN...

shut your mouth, here comes a bus. What you say to a child who has his/her mouth open. 'When I was a child my grandmother, if I had my mouth open in a typically idiotic gape, would say this' – Peter Toye (2000). 'Close your mouth, there's a bus coming' – in script of Carlton TV *Inspector Morse*, 'The Remorseful Day' (15 November 2000).

side. See AS AWKWARD...; SOMEBODY GOT OUT OF BED...

sign. See IT'S THE SIGN OF...

silence is golden, and you can't tell a sausage by its overcoat. 'My granny used to say, probably when we were a bit noisy, "Silence is golden, and you can't tell a sausage by its overcoat". I just thought you'd like to know' – Gillian Howard, Isle of Man (1994).

silent but deadly. Of a fart. From Helen Fielding, *Bridget Jones: The Edge of Reason*, Chap. 11 (1999): 'In aeroplane in sky. Having to pretend to be very busy wearing Walkman and writing as ghastly man next to self in pale brown synthetic-type suit keeps trying to talk to me in between silent but deadly farting.' Compare HAVE ITS CARPET SLIPPERS ON.

silk stockings. See ALL FUR COAT...

sin. See THERE ARE THREE SORTS OF...

sing before your breakfast, cry before your tea. 'To anyone who has the temerity to be cheerful in the morning' – Stella Richardson, Essex (1998). Apperson has a version of the more usual 'Sing before breakfast, cry before night' dating back to 1530.

sit. See GO AND SIT ON...; GO AND STAND UP...

(to) sit about like Joe Egg. From Peter Nichols, *A Day in the Death of Joe Egg*, Act 2 (1967): 'My grandma used to say, "Sitting about like Joe Egg," when she meant she had nothing to do.' Hence, the title of the play.

(to) sit like Piff(e)y. As when a person is left in an isolated, useless position for some time and asks, 'Why am I sat here like Piffy?' British North Country usage. A longer version is 'Sitting like Piffy on a rock-bun', remembered from the 1930s. And never send to ask who the original

Piffy was. 'When I was a lad in Macclesfield, sixty years ago, my mother often said to me: "Shape yourself, don't stand there like Piffey"' – John Heys, letter in the *Guardian* (17 August 1989). 'Waiting here like piffey' – Graham Whitehead (2000). Compare also: 'In the days before theme parks and garden centres, when it was quite usual to go for a Sunday picnic which included a visit to the family grave, a child in the party fell over and was comforted in these words: "sit on your grand-dad's grave and have a rock-bun". This phrase has been used ever since in our family as slightly mocking comfort, particularly if someone has been making an inordinate fuss about some minor mishap' – Glenys Hopkins, Cheshire (1994).

sit on your thumb but mind the nail. Fobbing-off phrase. 'When I was a child I remember that whenever one of us said, "Where shall I sit?" or "There's no seat for me", my parents used to reply...' – Wynne Kelly, West Midlands (1998). 'Recently I heard a relative of French Canadian origin say something in French when her children asked her what there was to eat. She said *"Mange ta main, et garde l'autre pour demain* [eat your hand and save the other for tomorrow]". So it's not only British parents who irritate their children!' (same source).

sixpence. See YOU CAN'T EXPECT...

skates. See COULD I POLISH...

skin. See ALL SKIN...; COULDN'T KNOCK...

(she'd) skin a lop for its tallow. 'Of a person sparing with food, my mother would say: "She'd skin a lop [flea] for its tallow"' – Mrs J. Payne, North Yorkshire (1995). Compare:

'My dear mother used a similar expression and as a young child in the 30s I was never quite sure what it meant – "She is *that* mean she would skin a flea for its hide and tallow"' – Rhena Stitt, Belfast (1996). Compare: 'My mother had a stock of the most original expressions from her dour Scottish upbringing. She would describe a Scrooge-like person as being: "So mean he'd skin a gnat for its hide"' – Travers Billington, Devon (1996). 'My grandmother's definition of false economy: "Someone would skin a gnat to save a farthing, and spoil a sixpenny knife to do it"' – B. Rouse, Worcestershire (1995).

sky blue pink with a finny haddy border. Fobbing-off phrase. 'This was my mother's invariable answer to any question when we were children' – Julie Hickson (2000). Compare 'sky-blue tail', 'bottom pink' and 'little thin flowery border' under NEAT BUT NOT GAUDY. Marjorie Wild, Devon recalled (2000) 'sky-blue-pink' and 'sandy-grey-russet' as nonsense descriptions. 'As a small child, when I asked an aunt what was the colour of something, she would teasingly reply, "Sky-blue scarlet, the colour of a mouse's fart" – to the annoyance of other adults. I have never heard this from anyone else, and have no idea whether or not it was my aunt's original' – Mrs J. Jones, Shropshire (1993). Well, Partridge/*Slang* has 'sky-blue pink' for 'colour unknown or indeterminate', since about 1885. Casson/Grenfell has, in answer to the question, 'What shall I wear?' – 'Sky blue pink.'

Skylark. See ANY MORE FOR THE...

skylight. See HAPPY AS A...

slap. See BETTER THAN...

(a) slice off a cut loaf is never missed. In other words, it doesn't matter having a bit on the side once you've taken the plunge and got married. In her autobiography, *Billie Whitelaw: Who He?* (1995), the actress recounts how her mother drew her aside when she was about to get married for the first time and told her to remember this bit of advice. 'After forty years I'm still trying to work out what she meant.' Well, I took it upon myself to tell her not so long ago! One has to say that it was an extraordinary thing for a mother to say on such an occasion. But it is a very old saying indeed. Apperson has it as 'It is safe taking a shive [= slice] of a cut loaf' and traces it back to Shakespeare, *Titus Andronicus*, II.i.87: 'What, man! more water glideth by the mill/Than wots the miller of; and easy it is/Of a cut loaf to steal a shive, we know.' Partridge/*Slang* has it that 'to take a slice' means 'to intrigue, particularly with a married woman.'

(a) slightest suspicion. 'My Grandmother's favourite saying at the dinner table, when she only wanted a small portion, was, "A slightest suspicion". No one ever asked why she said it but it still brings a laugh when all the family are together 25 years after her death' – Mrs W. Morton, Surrey (1996).

(she's got) slippery heels. 'Of a girl of easy virtue – a hussy (said with a sniff)' (Wickenden). Compare: 'she's got round heels' = 'she's anybody's, she's an easy lay' – a delightfully descriptive expression which suggests that a woman's heels are so curved that the slightest push from a man would put her on her back and in a position to have sexual intercourse. From the mid-20th century?

slow. See TOO SLOW TO CARRY HEAVY...

smack both – you'll get the right one then. 'On kids squabbling' (Wickenden). David Attenborough, the broadcaster, recalled on BBC Radio *Quote...Unquote* (6 April 1993): 'I had two brothers and we used to have a room in which we sort of, I suppose, used to *carry on*. We used to make a hell of a row, and we used to quarrel and one thing and another, and when it got too bad, my mother used to come in and she used to hit all three of us round the ear, "Clip-clip-clip". And then she used to say, "There you are. I've got one of the right ones this time!"'

smallest. See GO TO THE SMALLEST...; NICEST THINGS COME...

smell. See NO ONE EVER DIED OF A...; WHAT A SMELL OF BROKEN...

smells. See RAT SMELLS ITS OWN...

smoke. See YOU MIGHT AS WELL...

snake. See DRAIN ONE'S SNAKE...

snowball. See LIKE WHEN PUSSY BURNS...

snowing. See IT'S SNOWING...

snuff. See THROWING IT AROUND LIKE...

snug as a bug in a rug. Meaning 'well-fitting and/or extremely warm and comfortable'. Usually ascribed to Benjamin Franklin, the American writer and philosopher, who mentioned a type of epitaph in a letter to Miss Georgiana Shipley (26 September 1772) on the death of her pet squirrel, 'Skugg': 'Here Skugg lies snug/As a bug in a rug.' But there are earlier uses. In an anonymous work, *Stratford Jubilee* (commemorating David Garrick's Shakespeare festival in 1769), is: 'If she [a rich widow] has the mopus's [money]/I'll have her, as snug as a bug in a rug.' Probably, however, it was an established expression even by that date, if only because in 1706 Edward Ward in *The Wooden World Dissected* had the similar 'He sits as snug as a Bee in a Box' and in Thomas Heywood's play *A Woman Killed with Kindness* (1603) there is 'Let us sleep as snug as pigs in pease-straw.'

(he is) so mean he can peel an orange in his pocket. For some reason, I have a note of this expression as having being said by a 'Welsh woman 1920s/30s'.

(she's) so mean she wouldn't give you the dirt from under her finger nails. 'My mother' – Mrs Edna A. Smith, Isle of Wight (1995). Compare, from Casson/Grenfell: 'Look at your dirty finger-nails. Are we in mourning for the cat?'

(she's) so miserable that every time she laughs a donkey dies. 'My late father, John Berriman, used to say this of one particularly gloomy woman who lived in the next village to us in North Yorkshire' – Mrs Margaret Opie-Smith, London SE1 (1995).

(she's) so thin, she looks like a matchstick with the wood shaved off. 'On thinness' (Wickenden).

soap. See SACKED FOR EATING THE...

socks. See BLESS HIS LITTLE...; GO AND WRING...; HANDS OFF...

soldier. See THAT IS WHAT THE — SAID.

somebody got out of bed the wrong side today. I.e. 'you are in a temper'. Nannyism (Casson/Grenfell). Why this should have anything to do with the way you got out of bed is not clear. A more or less traditional saying: *Marvellous Love-Story* (1801) has, 'You have got up on the wrong side, this morning, George'; and Henry Kingsley, *Silcote of Silcotes* (1867) has, 'Miss had got out of bed the wrong side.'

soul. See KEEP BODY AND SOUL...

soup. See TO HELL WITH...

(to) spend a penny without paying anything. Loophemism. 'A friend of mine asked the Bobby on the beat, "Where can I spend a penny without paying anything?" The Bobby showed us the way' – Mrs Dorothy B. Alexander, Shropshire (1996). As for the basic phrase, 'to spend a penny', the first public convenience to charge one penny opened in London in 1855. So I am curious about this from Chapter 6 of Charles Dickens's *Dombey and Son* (1846–8): 'The young Toodles, victims of a pious fraud, were deluded into repairing in a body to a chandler's shop in the neighbourhood, for the ostensible purpose of spending a penny.' (*OED2* does not have a citation for the phrase before 1945.)

splash. See GO AND SPLASH...

spoil. See THEY'D SPOIL...

(a) sprat to catch a mackerel. 'Someone offering you a small favour in return for a big one' (Wickenden).

Apperson has 'giving a sprat to catch a herring' by 1827, and 'never to throw away sprats, but as bait for whales' in Charles Dickens, *Martin Chuzzlewit*, Chap. 8 (1850).

squeeze. See GO AND SQUEEZE...

stairs. See ALL STEPS...; I'LL GO TO THE FOOT...

stand. See DON'T STAND...; GO AND STAND UP...

(he was in the) Stand-Back Fusiliers. 'In the 1920s we had a neighbour who I thought must be the most patriotic man around. He flew the flag on every occasion and displayed photographs of the Royal Family. I asked my Dad who had been with the fusiliers from 1912–18 (when he was invalided out with severe wounds), if Mr X had been in his regiment. He said, "No, he was in the Stand-Back Fusiliers." I now realize it was a way of describing someone who, while fit for service avoided it' – Bill Lovett, Essex (1997). Partridge / *Slang* notes 'the Skin-Back Fusiliers' as 'a satirical attribution of a Serviceman's affiliation to an imaginary regiment or unit: WW2.'

(a) standing gatepost gathers no wisdom. 'Many years ago, in response to my father's repeating the well known, "a rolling stone gathers no moss", my grandmother came out with, "a standing gatepost gathers no wisdom". She certainly did not invent it, but I have never heard this saying since' – David Heal (1998). Compare 'standing pools gather filth', a proverb found by Apperson in 1639.

Sir Herbert Stanley. See APPROBATION FROM...

starvelings. See ARISE YE STARVELINGS...

starving. See THINK OF ALL THE POOR...

stay up till Dicky's dancing hour. 'When I was a child, my father, impressing on us the wisdom of going to bed early, would warn us: "Now, don't stay up till Dicky's dancing hour!" I'd love to know the origin. I'm 80' – Hilary Taylor, Hampshire (1995). I wonder if this could possibly have anything to do with dawn being the time when people are hanged? Sometimes this has been called 'the devil's dancing hour'. Or could the allusion be to hanged bodies dancing on the gibbet?

(they'd) steal the pennies off a dead man's eyes. 'Of the dishonest' – Stella Richardson, Essex (1998). Or 'they'd steal the eyes out of your head and come back for the sockets'. Compare: 'like taking money from blind beggars', meaning 'achieving something effortlessly, by taking advantage'; and 'as easy as taking/stealing pennies from a blind man' or 'sweets/ candy/money from a child'. 'Like taking candy from a baby' occurs in the film *Mr Smith Goes to Washington* (US 1939).

I first heard 'like taking money from blind beggars' in about 1962 – said by my English teacher who had just given a talk to a (wildly impressed) Women's Institute, or some such. But it is an old idea. Charles Dickens in *Nicholas Nickleby*, Chap. 59 (1838–9) has Newman Noggs say: 'If I would sell my soul for drink, why wasn't I a thief, swindler, housebreaker, area sneak, robber of pence out of the trays of blind men's dogs...'

steps. See ALL STEPS...

stewed eels and slow poison. Fobbing-off phrase. When asked what she was cooking for dinner, Mrs Greer would invariably reply this – as recounted by Germaine Greer on BBC Radio *Quote... Unquote* (1 June 1993).

sticks. See PEAS ABOVE STICKS.

stocking. See IT FITS LIKE...

stomach. See MY STOMACH THINKS...

stop. See ASK YOUR FATHER...; FACE WOULD STOP...

stop picking your nose – you've had your breakfast. Said by an RAF corporal and quoted by the father of Alice Wood (1985).

strain. See PUTTING AN EQUAL...

strawberries. See LIKE A DONKEY EATS...

strawberry. See OH LOOK, MAMA...

streak. See LIKE A STREAK...

streets. See NEVER LIKES TO GET UP...

strings. See ALWAYS PULL...

strong enough to trot a mouse on. 'My father, who was in the army for much of his life, always enjoyed a cup of tea but didn't like it too strong. If it was, he would remark that it was "strong enough to trot a mouse on"' – J.G. Hills, Hampshire (1994). The film director Bryan Forbes remembered this (1998) from Lincolnshire as 'strong enough for a mouse to skate on.'

struck. See DON'T STAND...

stuff. See THAT'S THE STUFF TO GIVE...

suck it and see. See ANSWER'S A LEMON.

sucking. See FIGHTING ONE MINUTE...

suffer. See YOU MUST SUFFER...

sufficiency. See ELEGANT...

suit the wearer, bugger the starer. 'Clothes criticism, when one wears what one likes' – Stella Richardson, Essex (1998).

summer. See YOU'VE GOT TO SUMMER...

Sundays. See NOT IN A MONTH OF...

suspicion. See SLIGHTEST SUSPICION...

swear. See IT'S ENOUGH TO MAKE...

swearing. See AS NEAR AS 'DAMN' IS TO...

sweat. See HORSES SWEAT...

sweep. See IT SHONE LIKE A...

sweet. See DRY BED...; GO FOR A SWEET...

system. See HAVE A GOOD CRY...

T

T.T.T. (Tummy Touching Table). Initial code. This was either a parental instruction not to eat more or an indication that one was so full that one could not eat more. Recalled by the broadcaster Joan Bakewell, from her Stockport childhood, on BBC Radio *Quote...Unquote* (24 May 1994).

table. See WHISPERERS AT THE TABLE...

tail. See ALL BEHIND...; IT'S BETTER TO HAVE...; WHO WILL LIFT THE DOG'S...

(to) take the maggot for a gallop. Loophemism – M.J. Langhurst, Surrey (1996).

tanner. See IT SHONE LIKE A...; LOOK LIKE YOU'VE LOST...

tap water. See LIKE A STREAK OF...

tea. See DON'T YOU POUR...; I WANT ME TEA; MILK?; MORE TEA, VICAR?; SING BEFORE YOUR BREAKFAST...

teapot. See GO AND EMPTY...

teeth. See LITTLE OLDER THAN MY . . . ; THEM AS 'ADN'T TEETH . . .

telephone. See GO AND TELEPHONE . . .

tell him to stick it up his backside to make a jug handle. 'Phrase for dealing with unwanted sexual advances' (Wickenden).

tell the truth and shame the Devil. (Wickenden). Apperson has this from one of Latimer's sermons (1552).

thank. See DON'T THANK . . .

that is what the — said. Dorothy M. Wolfe, Pennsylvania (1992) inquired about the phrase 'that is what the soldier said'. She did know the similar 'That is what the girl said' but with 'at the picnic' added. These are probably earlier versions of the more recent 'as / like the man said' or 'as the girl said to the sailor' which are both used as throwaway, humorous tags, though not quite to the subversive extent of 'as the bishop said to the actress'. Partridge / *Catch Phrases* suggests that the origin lies in the passage from Charles Dickens, *The Pickwick Papers*, Chap. 34 (1835–7) where Sam Weller remarks during the trial of Mr Pickwick, 'Oh, quite enough to get, sir, as the soldier said ven they ordered him three hundred and fifty lashes', and the judge interposes with, 'You must not tell us what the soldier, or any other man, said, sir… it's not evidence.'

(there') that'll stop you farting in church. 'This was the family saying that was invariably used by my father when he was obliged to act in order to prevent us youngsters from meddling with anything dangerous or from straying beyond control. He would place something beyond our reach or lock it away. He would say it to his ducks and chickens, too – and to himself when he considered that he had put right someone who had chanced their arm with him' – Jim Diston, Somerset (1994).

Partridge/*Catch Phrases* suggests that a politer form of this remark is 'that will stop him laughing in church' and that the original 'that will teach him to fart in chapel/stop their farting in chapel' (i.e. 'that'll stop them from taking liberties') is possibly an English public school expression of the 1930s.

that's another meal the Germans won't have. 'When my (French) wife arrived in this country some thirty years ago, she surprised me by remarking, after a particularly good meal, "*Voilà, un autre repas que les Allemands n' auront pas.*" This saying apparently derived from her mother, or indeed her grandmother, who suffered in the Occupation. To my astonishment, on a trip to Avignon ten years ago, after an exceptional banquet, a young French lad aged about 25, turned to my wife and made the same remark. It would seem that this has now become a French proverb' – Raymond Harris, London N1 (1995). Confirmation came from the *Sunday Times* (23 March 1997): 'Older Frenchmen admitted they sometimes still use the toast, when raising their glasses, of "This is one the *Boches* won't get".' And from even further back: 'On his first visit to Germany nearly forty years later, [Matisse] told one of his students that . . . he never forgot his mother repeating like a grace at meals: "Here's another one the Germans won't lay their hands on". The phrase would become a familiar refrain throughout the region during the incursions of the next seventy-five years and more' – Hilary Spurling, *The Unknown Matisse* (Vol. 1, 1998), referring to the Prussians who passed through north-eastern France in the 1871 Franco-Prussian war.

Compare: 'My grandmother used to say on seeing my nice clean plate after a meal (this was in the 1930s!): "That's gone where they don't play billiards"' – C.H. Filbey, Dorset (1995).

that's for me to know, and you to wonder. Fobbing-off phrase (Wickenden). Or, 'That's for me to know, and you to find out' – recalled by Jenni Murray on BBC Radio *Quote...Unquote* (3 April 2000).

that's just a few crows flying over. 'On a slight shower' – (Wickenden).

that's the stuff to give the troops. 'I remember people saying this in the 1940s when sitting down to eat ration-book food at home' – Norman Beaumont, Hampshire (1993). Partridge/ *Slang* actually dates this from the First World War but defines it simply as 'that's the idea, that's what we want', and not necessarily about food. There is an obvious allusion in P.G. Wodehouse, *Carry On, Jeeves*, 'The Spot of Art' (1930): 'Forgive me, old man, for asking you not to raise your voice. A hushed whisper is the stuff to give the troops.'

that's the worst of these cheap husbands. 'My mother always made this joke whenever things went wrong' – Bee Lancaster, Essex (1995).

them as 'adn't teeth gnashed their gooms! A quotation or what? – Mrs Wendy Eastaway, Co. Cork (1995). Jennifer Paterson, the chef, recalled her grandfather saying, also regarding teeth, 'Let 'em gnash 'em as have 'em' – on BBC Radio *Quote...Unquote* (2 May 1995)

them as finished first can help the others. 'My father would encourage his children to eat up quickly by urging this' – recalled by the broadcaster Joan Bakewell, from her Stockport childhood, on BBC Radio *Quote... Unquote* (24 May 1994).

there and back. See WHERE HAVE I BEEN?...

there are more ways of killing a cat than choking it with cream. This proverb was recorded by the mid-19th century (*CODP*). It appears as a nannyism in Casson/Grenfell. Compare 'There's more ways of killing a cat than choking it with strawberries' – contributed to BBC Radio *Quote... Unquote* (by 1980). 'My old dad used to say when tackling a building or electrical project, when the obvious approach was pointed out to him, "Aah, there's more ways of chokin' a pig than stuffin' it wi' butter"' – Austen Mitchell (2000). 'I was warned by a physiotherapist to take it easy with regard to sexual activity with the words, "There are more ways of killing a pig than blowing in its ear"' – Paul Jennings, Isle of Wight (2000).

there are no pockets in shrouds. 'My grandfather believed money was for hoarding, not spending. When budget discussions were about to become arguments, my grandmother would look him straight in the eye and with total conviction say, "George, there are no pockets in shrouds." This saying has become a household word' – Ena Constable, London N20 (1991). *CODP* has this as 'Shrouds have no pockets'. R.C. Trench, *On Lessons in Proverbs* (1854) refers to an Italian proverb: 'With an image Dantesque in its vigour, that "a man shall carry nothing away with him when he dieth", take this Italian, *Our last robe... is made without pockets.*'

there are three sorts of Sin – Little Ones, Bigger Ones, and Taking Off Your Shoes Without Undoing the Laces! Nannyism – included in Jonathan Gathorne-Hardy, *The Rise and Fall of the British Nanny* (1972).

there never were such times since Old Leather Arse died! 'When Grandma was alive, she would say this on auspicious occasions. As we all thought it rather rude, this later became "Never were such times...you know, since when!" No idea who Old Leather Arse was' – Jean Ford, Devon (1992).

Roger Trail, Dorset, subsequently recalled the version used by his grandfather, E.W. Westbrook (1877–1956): 'There never were such times since old Leather-arse fell out of the brake and busted the beano.' Mr Trail thought this must refer to an annual works outing of some kind (beano) by coach (brake): 'I suspect that the manager or some other member of the office staff would have been the natural target of such ribaldry. This is further reinforced by the definition of "leather-bottom" ("a Civil Servant tied to his desk") and "shiny-bum" ("to have a desk-job") in Eric Partridge's slang dictionary.'

'My aunt, from Framlingham, Suffolk, despite being quite proper would say, "I hadn't laughed (or, enjoyed myself) so much since old leather arse died' – E. Spratt, Hampshire (1998).

'there's a pair of you there,' said the devil to his horns. 'A saying of my Irish mother that covered anything from a couple of children misbehaving to adultery in high places' – Gerald Mason, Hampshire (1998).

there's life in the old dog yet. This expression of wonder may be uttered at the unexpected possession of some power by someone or some thing thought to be 'past it' (especially when referring to the person's love life). It was used as the title of a painting (1838) – precisely 'The Life's in the Old Dog Yet' – by Sir Edwin Landseer, which shows a Scottish ghillie rescuing a deerhound which, unlike a stag and two other hunting dogs, has not just plunged to its death over a precipice.

there's many a tune played on an old fiddle. 'On an old man with a young woman' (Wickenden). This proverb is probably better known in the form, 'There's many a good tune played on an old fiddle', which *CODP* finds first with a somewhat different slant: 'Beyond a haricot vein in one of my legs I'm as young as ever I was. Old indeed! There's many a good tune played on an old fiddle' – Samuel Butler, *The Way of All Flesh*, Chap. 61 (1902).

there's more knows Tom Fool than Tom Fool knows. As 'more know Tom Fool than Tom Fool knows' this is quoted as 'the old English proverb' in Daniel Defoe, *Colonel Jack*, Chap. 17 (1723). 'When my children were small and wondered how we knew some of the things that they did, the conversation would go: "How do you know?" – "There's a lot of people know Joe what Joe don't know"' – Mrs K. Polond, London SE23 (1995).

there's more out than in. 'On lunatics' (Wickenden).

there's only one look – and that's mine. 'If she was doing a job and you kept trying to look at it, she would say this' – (Wickenden).

they'd spoil another pair. 'I recall a particular saying of my Mother's which I have never heard voiced by anyone else. If ever she met up with a couple of rather unattractive appearance – i.e. husband and wife or newly-engaged pair – she would invariably say with a resigned air – "Oh, well – they'd spoil another pair"' – Margaret Baker, West Midlands (1992).

'When people commented adversely about a married couple, my grandfather would say, "Leave 'em alone – they'd have spoilt two good couples"' – Graham Whitehead, Lancashire (1997). 'An older lady when hearing that two people, both of unprepossessing appearance, were engaged to be married, was heard to say, "Well, they won't spoil two homes!"' – David Hine, Buckinghamshire (1998). 'My grandfather, a village blacksmith and farrier... was much given to making comments on people generally, and the one he would make on ill-favoured couples, was, "Well, at least it's not spoiling two households"' – R. Craggs, Hampshire (1998).

Compare the illustrious remark that Samuel Butler made about Thomas and Jane Carlyle (in a letter to Miss E.M.A. Savage, on 21 November 1884): 'It was very good of God to let Carlyle and Mrs Carlyle marry one another and so make only two people miserable instead of four...'

they're all mad but me and thee – and I've got my doubts about thee. 'My Father, who was part-Yorkshire, was fond of saying this' – Mrs Monica Nash, Nottinghamshire (1995). This is probably related to: 'All the world is queer save thee and me, and even thou art a little queer' – attributed to Robert Owen, the Welsh-born socialist reformer (1771–1858), on breaking up with his business partner, W. Allen, at New Lanark (1828).

thin. See SO THIN, SHE LOOKS LIKE...

**think of all the poor starving people in Africa/
China/India.** Nannyism. Wasn't it also advised that it was
polite to leave a little food on the side of the plate 'for the
starving in India' if not for 'Mr/Miss/Captain Manners'?
Paul Beale in Partridge/*Catch Phrases*, commenting on the
American expression 'Remember the starving Armenians',
notes: 'The one used to exhort me as a child, late 1930s, to
clear up my plate or to tackle something I found
unpalatable was "think of all the poor starving children in
China!"'

As for 'when people are starving in India...', I am
indebted to *The Complete Directory to Prime Time Network
TV Shows* (1981) for the information that when a proposed
US series called *B.A.D. Cats* crashed in 1980, Everett
Chambers, its executive producer, said, 'We bought
$40,000 worth of cars to smash up, and we never got a
chance to smash them up. I think that's kind of immoral,
$40,000 worth of cars to smash up when people are
starving in India.'

The nearest expression in Casson/Grenfell is, 'Think of
all the poor starving children who'd be grateful for that
nice plain bread and butter.'

(he/she) thinks his/her shit doesn't stink. 'On someone
who was stuck-up without reason' (Wickenden).
Partridge/*Catch Phrases* suggests that this expression has
been with us since about 1870. 'She thinks her shit don't
stink, but it do!' – grandmother of Graham Martin,
Ceredigion (2000).

this, and better, might do; this, and worse, will never do.
Informal proverb. 'My mother, Yorkshire born and bred,
when taking a break from her work, would always say:
"This, and better, might do; this, and worse, will never do."

"Do" of course means "be sufficient". Then she would resume her work' – June Fuller, Essex (1997). 'Years ago we had a neighbour who had a, as far as I know, unique saying. If you were sitting having a cup of tea in the middle of the morning and there was work still to be done, she would stand up and say, "Well, this and better *may* do; this and worse'll never." I still say it' – Gwyneth Harwood, North Yorkshire (1996).

(well) this is neither fishing nor mending nets. 'Grandmother getting out of her chair' – Mrs Monica van Miert, Tyne and Wear (1996). I.e. sitting here is not doing anything useful.

this won't bathe the baby. 'My mother, a very busy lady would sometimes sit down for a few minutes. Feeling guilty she would arise to these words (even though our baby days were long past). I still use it when there are things to be done' – Mrs Elizabeth Durham, Cheshire (1995). Compare: 'From my mother about time-wasting, "This won't get the children boots, or the baby a new bonnet"' – Deborah Chesshire, Somerset (1998). 'Well, this won't buy the baby new boots' (Wickenden). Casson/ Grenfell has the nannyism: 'Now I must get on, this will never get the baby a new coat.'

thought. See YOU KNOW WHAT...

(a) thousand a year or a handsome husband. Said when offering the last portion of food, last sandwich or last cake on a plate. Current in the 1950s, this saying now seems to promise rather slight remuneration for accepting the offer. Iona Opie and Moira Tatem in *A Dictionary of Superstitions* (1992) find various benefits linked to taking the last piece of food on a plate. Their earliest is a 'Lancashire legend' recalled in 1873. From 1923, in Kent: 'The person who, uninvited, takes the last slice of bread and butter from the plate will die unmarried. But the person who takes the last slice upon invitation will have a handsome spouse and an income of thousands amounting to the number of people at the table.' Sylvia Dowling, Lancashire (1998), wrote that in the 1950s it usually attracted the smart reply: 'I'll take the thousand a year and then I'll have my choice of handsome husbands.' See also DON'T SAY 'NO'...

thousands. See I BELIEVE YOU...

throat. See MY STOMACH THINKS...

throne. See GO AND SIT ON...

(he's) throwing his money about like a man with no arms. The traditional way of describing a mean person. Partridge/*Catch Phrases* has it as British/Australian since about 1930. Also 'flinging his money around...'

(she's) throwing it around like snuff at a wake. 'My elderly Irish aunt used to say this about people overly generous with their money' – Marie Hartshorne, Dorset (1994). Indeed, this is a pretty standard Irish expression. Partridge/*Catch Phrases* suggests it has been around since about 1910.

thumb. See SIT ON YOUR THUMB...

Thursday. See DON'T GO NO...

(you) tie that knot with your tongue which you can't undo with your teeth. 'I used to hear this from my grandfather, a Suffolk countryman' – Amalya Noël, Oxfordshire (1998). Referring to marriage, of course. Apperson finds this in John Lyly, *Euphues* (1580): 'We might knit that knot with our tongues, that we shall neuer vndoe with our teeth.'

tight as a duck's arse and that's watertight. 'On meanness' (Wickenden). Discussing the expression 'pissed as a newt' and, according to Partridge, the original 'tight as a newt', Paul Beale wrote to me in December 1987: 'The great thing about newts is the characteristic they share with fishes' arse'oles: they are watertight. And you can't get tighter than that!' I think one gets the drift.

tight cotton always breaks. 'Of quarrels between friends' – mother of Mrs Jean Wigget, Kent (1995).

time. See GO AND SEE WHAT...; WHAT'S THE TIME...

tinkers. See DISGRACE A FIELD...

to Hell with poverty, put another pea in the soup! 'We had a family saying that could be applied to any number of situations' – Janet Desmond, London NW5 (1995). Also from A.J. King, Suffolk (1998). 'The Ulster version of the poverty saying, used in our family was "To hell with poverty. Put another pea in the pan and give the cat a canary"' – June Fotheringame, Warwickshire (1998). Compare HANG THE EXPENSE...

Toby. See DON'T YOU SAY...

Tom Fool. See THERE'S MORE KNOWS TOM FOOL...

Tom Pepper. See YOU ARE A BIGGER...

tomorrow will be Friday. 'If as a child, disappointed over something, I gave a wail of "Ooh!", my father would join in with, "Ooh! Tomorrow will be Friday and we've caught no fish today". I don't know the origin of this, but I think it must be a song of the Edwardian era. Comic opera perhaps? Is there one about monks?' – Joan Bell, Clackmannanshire (1992).

Well, there is a song about monks failing to catch fish for Friday consumption and resorting to the bottle instead. It is called 'Tomorrow Will Be Friday' and has words by Fred E. Weatherly to music by James Lyman Molloy, who died in 1900, thereby putting its composition sometime in the 1890s:

> The sun was setting and vespers done,
> From chapel the monks came one by one,
> And down they went thro' the garden trim,
> In cassock and cowl to the river's brim...
>
> So down they sate by the river's brim,
> And fish'd till the light was growing dim,
> They fish'd the stream till the moon was high,
> But never a fish came wand'ring by.
>
> They fish'd the stream in the bright moonshine,
> But not one fish would come to dine;
> And the abbot said 'It seems to me,
> These rascally fish are all gone to sea!
> And tomorrow will be Friday,
> But we've caught no fish today...'

There are also paintings by the English artist Walter Dendy Sadler (1854–1923) entitled 'Thursday' and 'Friday', depicting comparable events. The first of these (in the Tate Britain gallery) *may* also have been known as 'Tomorrow Will Be Friday', though it was painted in 1880 and thus precedes the song.

tongue. See CAT GOT YOUR...; LITTLE OLDER THAN MY...; YOU'LL NEVER GET LOST...

'too late, too late!' shall be the cry... This seems to be the basis of a series of fairly nonsensical expressions, uttered when some opportunity has been missed. 'Too late, too late, shall be the cry,/Arnold the ice-cream man's gone by' is to be found in the Peter Nichols play *The Freeway*, Act 1, Scene 3 (1974). 'My father, who is from the West of Ireland, says: "Too late, too late, will be the cry,/When the man with the oranges has passed by"' – from an anonymous correspondent (1995). Alison Klenar (2000) recalled from her childhood, '"Too late, too late," the maiden cried,/"I'd rather have my haddock fried!"'

Compare what Partridge/*Catch Phrases* calls originally a military catchphrase – 'Too late! too late!' spoken in a high falsetto, after the story of 'that luckless fellow who lost his manhood in a shark-infested sea very soon after he had summoned help.' Another possible origin: John Gray of Sutton wanted to know (1993) the source and correct form of a couplet that his father used to quote at him when he was a boy:

> Too late, too late, shall be the cry
> When you see — passing by.

Sir David Hunt suggested that this was probably a corruption of a hymn to be found in the Sankey and Moody hymnal. Indeed, the final couplet of the concluding verse of 'Jesus of Nazareth passeth by' by Miss Etta Campbell and T.E. Perkins is:

> 'Too late! too late!' will be the cry –
> 'Jesus of Nazareth *has passed by.*'

This came as a revelation to Stuart Holm of Norwich, who recalled living in Morecambe when he was a student at Lancaster University in the late 1960s. 'A regular Sunday ritual was a stroll along the promenade with a few fellow students. Among the delights on offer, a street trader was usually to be found selling a variety of wares to the accompaniment of the inevitable sales patter. He adapted "Too late, too late" as part of his sales pitch, leading on one memorable occasion to the unforgettable phrase, "Too late, too late will be the cry, when the man with the gents fully automatic umbrella passes you by." Umbrella was pronounced "umbarella" and the overall effect so amused my friend Ross Reynolds and I that it became a catchphrase for the rest of our time at university.'

Llywela V. Harris, Dyfed (1994), remembered from her childhood the pithier 'Too late, too late, the pawnshop's shut!' Jaap Engelsman, Amsterdam, noted (1996): 'A well-known Dutch catchphrase is *Te laat, te laat, sprak Winnetou, het zaad is al naar binnen toe* (or *Helaas, helaas, sprak...*), meaning "'Too late, too late (Alas, alas)' spoke Winnetou, the sperm's gone in already." The Red Indian Winnetou appeared from 1893 onwards in a series of very popular novels by the German author Karl May (1842–1912).'

'too late, too late!' the — cried and waved his/her wooden leg. Obviously related to the previous phrase. T.A. Dyer, London SW12, noted (1993) that his father used to say (in the 1940s): '"It's come too late!" the lady cried, as she waved her wooden leg – and passed out.' In about 1984, an American professor queried the saying, '"Aha!" cried she, as she waved her wooden leg, and died' – which is clearly linked. '"Too late, too late," the maiden cried/Lifted her wooden leg, and died' – Mrs. K.W. Kent, Lancaster (1994). Donald Hickling, Northamptonshire, recalled a nonsense poem that his father brought back from the First World War which included the phrase, 'Waving her wooden leg in dire despair.' He added that his family would exclaim it whenever a disaster-prone neighbour hammered on the party wall. P.S. Falla, the translator, wrote (1996): 'There is, "Ha, ha" she cried in Portuguese/And waved her wooden leg." I have heard the first line of this in French also!' 'This saying I have only heard via my mother, and she is 86: "'Oh good,' she said, as she swung her wooden leg, 'only one boot to clean'" – from Margaret Addicott, Hertford-shire (1996). Remembered by Rip Bulkeley, Oxfordshire (1998), from an American source: 'Ha Ha! she cried, waving her wooden leg. Only one shoe to clean.' But also from his Yorkshire granny fifty years ago: '"Help! Help!" she cried, and waved her wooden leg.' '"Aha! cried the Duchess, as she waved her wooden leg", also the variant, "Oho! she cried, as the cock flew at her" were both used as jokey exclamations by our Nanny (born 1897), and we were so used to hearing them as children in the 1950s that we never questioned her about where they came from' – Nick Bicat, Oxfordshire (2000).

'Too late! Too late! the Captain cried, and shook his wooden leg' – Tom Doyle, Madrid, Spain. Adam Wilkins, St Albans (2000), remembered from his grandfather, '"Too late, too late," she cried as she waved her wooden leg three times in the air.' '"Too late, too late", the maiden cried, as she waved her timber limber' – remembered by the mother of Marjorie Wild, Devon (2000). '"'Oh, thank you, sir,' she said, as with a smile she waved her wooden leg" – heard from my father and only once heard from another man at work' – Derek Armstrong (2000).

Clearly, the cry is not 'too late, too late' in all versions, but the emphasis remains upon the wooden leg, as in these citations from the US: '"Aha!" she cried, as she waved her wooden leg and died' – Anonymous, 'Some Wellerisms from Idaho' in *Western Folklore* 25 (1966); '"Hurrah!" as the old maid shouted waving her wooden leg' – Herbert Halpert, 'Some Wellerisms from Kentucky and Tennessee' in *Journal of American Folklore*, No. 69 (1956).

(I'm) too light for heavy work now. 'On being asked for a light' (Wickenden).

(you're) too slow to carry cold puddings to a dead man's funeral. 'Of a slow person' – recalled from a junior school teacher by Sue Ould (2000). Compare: 'He's too slow to catch a cold' (Wickenden). Partridge/*Catch Phrases* merely records the less elaborate 'too slow to go to a funeral'.

topmost. See GIVE SOMEONE THE...

touches. See FITS WHERE IT...

toys. See DIFFERENCE BETWEEN...

treacle. See PUT ONE'S PUDDINGS...; WHIMWAM FOR A GOOSE'S BRIDLE...

troops. See THAT'S THE STUFF TO GIVE...

trouble. See NEVER TROUBLE TROUBLE...

troubles. See FULL OF . . . ; LET'S HAVE A CUP OF TEA . . .

trousers. See ALL MOUTH . . . ; ENOUGH BLUE . . .

(his) trousers have had a row with his boots. 'When there is a gap between someone's trouser bottoms and boots' (Wickenden).

true. See HOW TRUE THAT IS . . .

true, O King! Shortly after I got married in 1978, I noticed that if I made an obvious statement, perhaps even a pompous one, my wife had a way of saying to me, 'True, O King!' I wondered where she had picked this up from until one day I happened to see some old film of Charles Laughton indulging in a spot of public reading from the Bible, as he was latterly wont to do. He was telling the story of Nebuchadnezzar and the gentlemen who were cast into the burning fiery furnace, from Daniel 3:24. Nebuchadnezzar asks, 'Did not we cast three men bound into the midst of fire?' – 'They answered and said unto the king, True, O king.' So that was it.

The nearest Shakespeare gets is the ironical '"True"? O God!' in *Much Ado About Nothing*, (IV.i.68), though he has any number of near misses like 'true, my liege', 'too true, my lord' and 'true, noble prince'.

Just to show that my wife is not alone – Mrs H. Joan Langdale, Kent, told me (1998), 'My father, a Classical Scholar and an Anglican priest, used to use your wife's quotation "True, O King!" and always added, "Live for ever".' See also OH KING LIVE FOREVER.

trumpeter. See WHAT DID YOUR LAST TRUMPETER DIE OF?

trunk. See UNPACKING YOUR...

trust in the Lord ... and keep your bowels open. Father of Doris Humphrey, Lincolnshire (1995). Compare the advice, reported in Partridge/*Catch Phrases*, to someone joining the Army (around 1920), 'Keep your bowels open, your mouth shut, and never volunteer!'

trust in the Lord ... and tie up your camel. My wife told me this one, having heard it in a business context. Mrs Joan Tompkinson, Devon (1998), whose father served in the First World War, remembers him saying: 'Put thy trust in Allah, but tie up thy camel thyself.'

truth. See TELL THE TRUTH AND SHAME...

Tuesday. See IT'S THE LAST...

tune. See THERE'S MANY A TUNE...

(that's the) tune the old cow died of. 'Of a poorly sung song' – Stella Richardson, Essex (1998). Partridge/*Catch Phrases* interprets this as 'that's a damned unpleasant noise!' and finds it in Captain Marryat, *Mr Midshipman Easy* (1836) and later in Mark Twain, *Life On the Mississippi* (1883). Apperson, as ever, finds it even earlier in Thomas Fuller, *Gnomologia*, No. 4360 (1732): 'The tune the old cow died of, that is the old tune upon the bag-pipe.'

Turk. See GO AND SEE THE TURK...

turn. See GO AND TURN...

turn 'Erbert's face to the wall. What you say when someone is deemed to have brought shame on himself. TV football commentator Jimmy Hill commented, 'Turn Albert's face to the wall, mother', after the Belgian player Philippe Albert cost his side a goal in the 1994 World Cup. John Gould, Denis Norden, Steve Race and Claire Rayner rushed to tell me that this was an allusion to the 1935 comic song, 'Turn 'Erbert's face to the wall, Mother,/Never more mention his name,/For he's brought disgrace on the family,/And bowed down our heads in shame.' With words and music by William Ellis, Max Kester and Ronald Hill, it was popularised by Gracie Fields.

'twas ever thus! An exclamation of mild despair at some example of inefficiency or incompetence and meaning almost the same as the modern 'So what's new?' It does not occur in Shakespeare or the Bible. In fact, the only examples I have turned up (and without the fatalistic edge) are: as the first line of 'Disaster' by C.S. Calverley (died 1884), ''Twas ever thus from childhood's hour!' (this is a parody of lines from Thomas Moore's 'The Fire Worshippers' in *Lalla Rookh* (1817): 'Oh! ever thus, from childhood's hour!'; and, as the title, ''Twas Ever Thus' given to a parody of the same poem by Henry S. Leigh (1837–83). His version actually begins, 'I never rear'd a young gazelle...'

twins. See DON'T YOU POUR...

two jumps at the pantry door and a bite off the latch. Fobbing-off phrase 'in response to someone asking what the next meal is' – Stella Richardson, Essex (1998). 'What's for dinner? Three jumps at the pantry door and four if you're hungry' – John Titford in an article from his column in *Family Tree Magazine* (December 1994).

two six. See DO A TWO SIX.

U

(the) ugliest man is worthy of the most beautiful woman. 'My late Mother used to say this to me when I was "coming out" (i.e. growing up) and she feared I would be left "on the shelf"' – Stella Fry, London NW3 (1996).

ugly. See YOU'RE BIG ENOUGH...

ugly enough to eat oats. 'My mother – now gone from us – used to say of startlingly ill-favoured people that they were "ugly enough to eat oats". Very expressive, I think, but I never asked her if this was an original expression' – John Francis, Hampshire (1995). Presumably a variation of 'with a face like horse'. Apperson finds 'ugly enough to wean a foal' in *Cheshire Proverbs* (1917).

uncle. See BOB'S YOUR UNCLE!

underclothes. See ALL OVER...

(I see you're) unpacking your trunk. 'My father had an admonition that I have never forgotten. If he saw any of us young children picking our noses he would say, "You're staying then? I see you're unpacking your trunk"' – Bill Shuard, Co. Antrim (1992).

up. See DIDN'T COME UP...

up and down like a fiddler's elbow. 'Mum, exasperated with her small son (me), who would keep running in and out and chasing up and down stairs, "Stay put, dammit. Up and down like a fiddler's elbow"' – Ray Dudley, London E17 (1994).

Indeed, 'like a fiddler's elbow' was quite a general expression and had been recorded by 1887. Martin Ward, Norfolk, commented (1994): 'The richness of this simile is its more metaphorical (and more common) use. I have always heard it used to describe something which is not in motion – for instance, the uneven ridge of a house – something which deviates from the horizontal plane.

'Other builders' expressions include: "Hard as a whore's heart" (e.g. concrete, wood) and, for things which do actually move up and down, "Up and down like a whore's drawers".'

up in Annie's room behind the clock. My wife recalled her mother using this phrase in the 1950s. Colleen Spittles, Kent, preferred (1993), 'Up in Annie's room behind the wallpaper' for when 'something had disappeared, who knows where.'

Partridge/*Slang* simply has 'Up in Annie's room' as a services' catchphrase from before the First World War, in reply to a query concerning someone's whereabouts. Partridge/*Catch Phrases* has 'Up in Annie's room behind the clock' as the civilian version of this.

(to lead someone) up/down the garden path. Meaning 'to trick or deceive' and current by the 1920s, certainly. One origin I have come across is that it dates from the 19th century, when you would take a person up or down the garden path to a shady bower which provided cover for seduction. Sue Limb, who entitled a newspaper column and book *Up the Garden Path*, commented (2000): 'The friend who suggested the title to me thought it encapsulated ideas of fruitfulness and deception. I suppose in the past the garden was the only place where courting couples could attain a degree of privacy. Jane Austen's hero and heroine always adjourn to the shrubbery at moments of maximum amorous tension. The absence of witnesses or eavesdroppers also means, I suppose, that heartless seducers could get away with breaking promises made in rosy bowers – hence, "He's leading you up the garden path". I wonder if it is related to the Primrose Path of Dalliance? Or, indeed, Tip-toeing through the Tulips?'

However, there is strong support for the idea that the trick was originally being played on a *pig*. 'I have always understood the phrase originated in the days when what would then have been regarded as the lower orders kept a domestic pig or two. When it came time for slaughter – away from the eyes of the children – the luckless pig would be led, quite literally up the garden path to the shed or other out-house to meet its fate – thus the impression conveyed by the expression that one was being led in complete innocence toward something highly undesirable' – Laurence Fowler (2000). 'When I was evacuated to a farm labourer's cottage in Oxfordshire in 1940, I was told by a slaughterman that "Led by the nose, up the garden path and over the garden wall" had regard to the last five minutes of a pig's life – a performance which I witnessed. No humane killing then!' – Roy Bartlett (2000). A description of the somewhat messy procedure is to be found in Thomas Hardy, *Jude the Obscure*, Chap. 10 (1895), though the phrase is not used.

up the wooden hill/stairs to Bedfordshire. Originally a nursery euphemism, I think this has become part of grown-up 'golf-club slang', as someone once termed it – i.e. a conversational cliché. Casson/Grenfell include it as a nannyism, together with 'Come on, up wooden hill, down sheet lane'. 'Up the Wooden Hill to Bedfordshire' was the title of the very first song recorded by Vera Lynn, in 1936. The 'bed – fordshire' joke occurs in a synopsis of *Ali Baba and the Forty Thieves; or, Harlequin and the Magic Donkey* staged at the Alexandra Theatre, Liverpool, in 1868. Indeed, as so often, Jonathan Swift found it even earlier. In *Polite Conversation* (1738), the Colonel says, 'I'm going to the Land of Nod.' Neverout replies: 'Faith, I'm for *Bedfordshire.*' But then again, the poet Charles Cotton had used it in 1665 and Apperson finds 'Bedfordshire' = 'bed' in a play by Middleton in 1608.

Jim Sweeney, the comedy performer, recalled on BBC Radio *Quote…Unquote* (10 May 1994) that not only would his mother say the above, his father would set off early to bed with the words: 'I will arise and go now, and go to Innisfree' (courtesy of W.B. Yeats).

upstairs. See GO UPSTAIRS.

V

vaccinated with a gramophone needle. 'Of a chatterbox' – Mrs D.M. Broom, Berkshire (1996). In fact, this is a quotation. In the film *Duck Soup* (US 1933), Groucho Marx says to Margaret Dumont: 'You know, you haven't stopped talking since I came here. You must have been vaccinated with a phonograph needle.'

vegetables. See WHAT ARE THE THREE...

vestry. See JUST IN TIME...

vicar. See GO AND SEE THE VICAR...; MORE TEA, VICAR?

vinegar. See LOOK LIKE THEY HAD BEEN...

(to have) vinegar on a fork. 'To be sharp or scary' (Wickenden).

virtue. See PATIENCE IS A VIRTUE...

W

wagon-load. See CRAFTY AS...

wait-and-see pudding. Fobbing-off phrase in answer to 'What's for dinner?' – Marjorie Wild, Devon (2000). Mrs Tickner, Surrey, was 84 in 1994 when she wrote to say that this was also what mum would reply when asked, 'What have we for pudding?' Compare 'Patience pudding with wait-a-while sauce' – a nannyism in Casson/Grenfell.

waits. See EVERYTHING COMES...

want never gets. 'If one said, "I want...", we would be told: "Want never gets" or "Want will be your master"' – Miss O.E. Burns, West Midlands (1995). Casson/Grenfell has, rather, 'I want gets nothing'.

(she) wants to know the ins and outs of a nag's arse. 'As my long departed Mum used to declare when talking about someone unduly inquisitive: "She wants to know the ins and outs of a nag's arse." The expression has not been lost with her passing!' – Eric Silvester, Wiltshire (1995). 'My grandmother (born around 1890) met any child's inquisitive questions with "You want to know the ins and outs of Mag's behind"' – David Coles, London N21 (1998). 'Mag's' would seem to be a softer substitution for 'nag's'. Or possibly 'magpies', as 'you would want to know the ins and outs of a magpie's bottom' has also been recorded. Compare INS AND OUTS OF A MERRYMAN'S BACKSIDE.

(he) wants waiting on hand and foot – with two helpings of foot. 'My mother often used to say this' – Bryn Strudwick, Hampshire (1996).

wash. See GO AND WASH...

washed. See HEAVENS, ELEVEN...

watch. See YOU'RE AS DAFT...

water. See GO AND WATER...; LIKE THE BARBER'S CAT...

we are not here for ease and sin but manhood's noble crown to win... 'My schoolteacher father-in-law's admonition' – Stephen Willis, Cheshire (1996). This is a quotation from the hymn 'Go Forth to Life' (1894) written by Samuel Longfellow, brother of H.W.:

> Go forth to life, O child of earth,
> Remembering still thy heavenly birth,
> Thou art not here for ease or sin,
> But manhood's noble crown to win.

we can't all and some of us don't. 'When one of the family makes a hash of something, we say this resignedly' – Mrs Heather Gibling, Devon (1996).

we do not necessarily improve with age...Informal proverb. Sir Peter Hall, the English theatre director, was quoted in the *Observer* (about 1988) as saying: 'We do not necessarily improve with age: for better or worse we become more like ourselves.' In fact, this was almost a proverbial expression by then. In my *Eavesdroppings* (1981), I quoted this from Miss Bernice Hanison of Haywards Heath: 'On the London Underground, I heard one of those carrying, well-bred, female voices saying to her companion: "I don't know about you, but as we get older I always find we get more and more like ourselves".'

we shall have to eke it out, as the girl did her manners. 'My mother brought us up – a family of six boys – in the hard times of the 1930s. When the food supply ran low, she would say this' – A.G. Foot, Norfolk (1994).

we'll hope so in case not. 'When anxious about something, my Gran always said this' – Mrs D. Barker, Staffordshire (1997).

(well) we's all live till we dee, unless dogs worries us. 'This was used by my mother – a Yorkshire West Riding lady – usually after some minor disaster in the home' – Kit Blease, Merseyside (1992). Anne Gledhill, West Yorkshire, added (1993): 'It was part of my background, too (born and brought up in Dewsbury in the West Riding). My version: "We shall live till we dee – if t'dogs doesn't worry us" (the second part given an ironic twist).' Apperson finds this particular expression in *Lancashire Sayings* (1901): 'We shan o live till we dee'n – iv th' dogs dunno wory us', but in Richard Jefferies, *Field and Hedgerow* (1889): 'The old country proverb, "Ah, well, we shall live till we die if the pigs don't eat us, and then we shall go acorning".'

wearer. See SUIT THE WEARER...

weary. See WHERE THE WICKED CEASE...

weather. See LOVELY WEATHER FOR...

wedding. See IT'S A MONKEY'S...

wee. See GO FOR A WEE...

week. See IT'S THE LAST...

well. See ONE O' THEM AS IS EITHER...

well done – you'll never see what I'll buy you. 'When we had done well, this is what my father would say. We had visions of fabulous gifts – till we got older and worked it out' – Mrs Edna A. Smith, Isle of Wight (1995).

wet. See FEEL LIKE A BUS...; MACKEREL SKY IS...

wet and warm. On being offered a drink, one might say, 'I don't mind what it is, so long as it's wet and warm.' Almost a conversational cliché. H.L. Mencken in his *Dictionary of Quotations* (1942) cites a 'Dutch proverb': 'Coffee has two virtues: it is wet and warm.' Pat Tomalin, Dorset (1992), related how in Kenya (about 1950), 'We used to say, "Wet and warm, like a honeymoon in Aden".'

what a name to go to bed with. 'It was New Year's Eve 1943. I was a Cypher Officer W.R.N.S. on watch at midnight. I was introduced to a man called Worthington Edridge. "Oh," I said, "What a name to go to bed with" (current remark at the time). He said, "Nobody asked you". I don't think you can beat that for a put down' – Mrs

D.M. Heigham, Hampshire (1993). Partridge/*Slang* has 'a nice name to go to bed with', meaning 'an ugly name', dating from 1887 and compares the French expression, '*Un nom à coucher dehors*'. Presumably, this originated with the nannyism (as in Casson/Grenfell): 'What a *face* to go to bed with.'

what a nice new one, made out of Daddy's old one. 'One of my old granny's sayings was – when a baby boy was born, she would look at his little willy and say...' – Mrs J. Collins, East Sussex (1998).

what a smell of broken glass! 'When driving in the country pre-war, with its appropriate smells around farms, my father always used to say this' – Jocelyn Linter, Essex (1998). Partridge/*Slang* has 'smell of broken glass – a strong body-odour, e.g. in a Rugby footballers' changing-room after a game...earlier C20' and compares 'there's a smell of gunpowder – someone has broken wind, late C19.' But how does glass come into it?

what a world it is for woossit... 'I had a country-bred Grandmother and her sayings are now part of family lore. My own grandchildren hear me using them, so the phrases go on in time, especially, "What a world it is for woossit, and nobody knows how to knit" (and all are baffled by the word "woossit")' – Mrs F. Smith, West Yorkshire (1993).

Vera Geddis, Hampshire, misheard this last as 'What a world this is for worsted' and was reminded of a saying of her mother's: 'What a world this is for worsted, fourteen balls of cotton for a penny!' She added: 'I cannot recall my mother ever explaining her saying – I am not certain whether the number of balls was fourteen or sixteen – but I assume that the point of it was that when tempted to bewail the state of the world, one cheered oneself up by changing it into a statement about the amazing cheapness of worsted.' Indeed, Wright's *English Dialect Dictionary* (1900) gives 'worset' as a form of 'worsted', so there seems to be more than the glimmer of an explanation here.

what are the three rudest vegetables?/Turn up and lettuce, pea! (Wickenden).

what are you looking at? 'If someone obnoxious said, "What are you looking at?", you replied: "I don't know, they don't put labels on rubbish"' (Wickenden).

what did your last servant die of? 'My mother, Iris Toeman, when one of the children was being lazy about (e.g.) carrying something, used to say this' – Richard Toeman, London N6 (1995). Partridge/*Catch Phrases* has this as 'used when someone asks you to do something he could easily do himself' and 'when did your last servant die?' as meaning 'don't order me about'. Also 'who was your lackey last year?' as 'I'm not a servant – do it yourself' by 1840.

what did your last trumpeter die of? 'When boasting occurred' – mother of Marjorie Wild, Devon (2000). Compare what actress Diana Quick said (1993) of her Irish mother-in-law, Kate: 'If people were getting above themselves and boastful, she would say: "I saw a shabby funeral. They need a trumpeter".' This echoes the old saying, addressed to an egotist, 'Your trumpeter is dead', which Apperson finds by 1729. From Baker's *Northamptonshire Glossary* (1854): 'Sometime it is said [again to an egotist], "your trumpeter's dead", i.e. no one sounds your praises, so you are compelled to extol yourself.' Casson/Grenfell has the nannyisms: 'Who's lost his trumpeter?' and: 'I thought I saw a shabby funeral going down the road.'

what do you expect from a pig but a grunt? 'To someone who has been verbally offensive' – Stella Richardson, Essex (1998). Partridge/*Catch Phrases* finds a citation for this in 1918 and asserts, reasonably, that this saying must have been prompted by the proverb 'You can't make a silk purse out of a sow's ear.'

what seems like despair may be mainly dirt – have a good wash. 'My grandmother (nine children, one outside tap) had this saying, I have been told' – Miss C.S. Woodard, East Sussex (1998).

what you don't have, you don't have to thank for. 'If someone had not given you something you hoped for' (Wickenden).

what'll not fatten'll fill. 'When dishing up a war-time meal which she did not consider to be of her usual standard' – grandmother of Stella Richardson, Essex (1998).

'what?'s dead long ago and 'pardon?' took its place – said to person who asks 'What?' Nannyism. In script of Carlton TV *Inspector Morse*, 'The Remorseful Day' (15 November 2000).

what's that got to do with the —? Meaning 'what you've just said is irrelevant.' 'When I was a child in Canada, the expression commonly used was, "What's that got to do with the price of tea in China?"' – Reg Norman, Somerset (2000). Also: 'What has that to do with Bacchus?' which

Brewer's Dictionary of Phrase and Fable (1989) finds in classical literature. Partridge/*Catch Phrases* has 'What's that got to do with the price of eggs?' as being of American origin. Sir Joh Bjelke-Peterson, Premier of Queensland, was reported in *The Australian* (1 May 1985) as saying of something he thought was irrelevant, 'That's got nothing to do with the price of butter.' 'What's that got to do with the price of fish?' – Jane Bird, North Yorkshire (2000), quoting a friend. 'What's that got to do with the Prince of Wales?' – told to me on an LBC radio phone-in, London (1990), but otherwise untraced and unconfirmed. And which Prince of Wales was being talked about, unless this is a simple price/prince play on words?

'When my children were young and far from clean and tidy, I would say, "The state of you and the price of fish!"' – Patricia Harrison, Hertfordshire (1999).

what's that when it's at home? 'On an unusual name' (Wickenden). Partridge/*Catch Phrases* has this as a tag 'implying either derision or incredulity' and has a citation from 1914.

what's the time?/knickers on the line. In our household, when someone asks, 'What's the time?' and the answer happens to be (as it does, frequently, for some reason), 'Half past nine,' the first person says, 'Knickers on the line.' One of a number of ritual additions, this was imported by my wife from her Buckinghamshire childhood of the 1950s. In a section called 'Crooked Answers' in *The Lore and Language of Schoolchildren* (1959), Iona and Peter Opie print two versions of a rhyme from Alton, Hampshire:

What's the time?
Half past nine
Put the napkins on the line.
When they're dry
Bring them in
And don't forget the safety pin.

And:

What's the time?
Half past nine
Hang your breeches on the line.
When the copper
Comes along
Pull them off and put them on.

what's worse than eating an apple and finding a maggot?/Eating an apple and finding half a maggot. 'Still crops up when eating fruit' – Marian Horner, Cambridgeshire (1998).

wheat. See GO AND CHECK THE PRICE...

when I says 'Fix', you don't fix, but when I says 'Bayonets', you whips them out and whops them on (and all I want to see is a flash of steel and a line of living statues). The army command 'fix...bayonets!' gave rise to this much-repeated spiel from an NCO teaching his squad to obey it. It was recalled (from over 50 years ago) by George Alexander, London SW15 (1998), and it refers to the old Lee Enfield rifle, not the modern type you can't put down. Also recalled by Peter Burke, Hampshire (1998), after Bill Cotton had recalled on BBC Radio *Quote...* *Unquote* that his father, the band-leader Billy Cotton, also used to say it.

when I was your age... One of Denis Norden's list of old person's phrases, recalled on BBC Radio *Quote...Unquote* (21 May 1996).

when it's brown it's done, when it's black it's buggered. 'On baking something' (Wickenden). Indeed, Peter Cotterill of Doncaster wrote to the *Guardian* (28 March 1987) and quoted his Lancashire mum to this effect. Paul Beale found this in Alec Dixon, *Tinned Soldier: A Personal Record (1919–1926)*, Chap. 9 (1941) – of life in the Royal Tank Corps and the methods of the cook house staff: 'Theirs was a system of trial and error and they were governed only by the time-honoured principle that "when it's brown it's cooked; when it's black it's mucked".'

when Nelson gets his eye back. 'If some plan was impossible to fulfill, we would be told it could come about in this unlikely event' – Miss O.E. Burns, West Midlands (1995). Also recalled as a fobbing-off phrase, when a child asks the question, 'When?' – Stella Richardson, Essex (1998).

when one door closes another door closes. A cynical variant (which I first heard in 1969) of the old 'Irish proverb' (according to H.L. Mencken, *A Dictionary of Quotations*, 1942), 'God never shuts one door but He opens another.' Whether Irish or not, *CODP* has it as already proverbial by 1586. Casson/Grenfell has the nannyism: 'When God shuts a door he always opens a window.' The cynical variant also comes – perhaps more usually – in the form 'as one door closes, another door shuts'.

when poverty comes in at the door, love flies out of the window. A full-blooded proverb. *CODP* first finds something like it in 1631, though Caxton had as 'a comyn prouerbe in englond that lue lastest as longe as the money endurith' in 1474. Later citations include: 'Still want had never yet come in at the door to make love for these innocents fly out at the window' – Elizabeth Gaskell, *Mary Barton*, Chap. 7 (1848); when a woman says, 'I don't like this innuendo', in the film *Monkey Business* (US 1931), Groucho Marx replies: 'That's what I always say. Love flies out the door when money comes innuendo.' There is a parallel proverb (known since 1605): 'Love comes in at the window and goes out at the door.'

when the fields are white with daisies, I'll return. 'My late father, on leaving the house, or even a room, for a short time, used to say, rather pompously: "I go: and when the fields are white with daisies, I shall return." Was this a quotation, if garbled?' – Alison M. Deveson, Hampshire (1995). The translator P.S. Falla recalled that the expression was used 'near the beginning' of one of P.G. Wodehouse's 'Psmith' novels. Could it have been *Psmith in the City* (1910)? Well, yes it could, in Chapter 6: 'No, he has not gone permanently. Psmith will return. When the fields are white with daisies he'll return.' But what was the allusion? Well, there was a song entitled 'When the Fields Are White With Daisies'. In fact, there is more than one, but the version published in 1904 has words and music by the Americans C.M. Denison and W.A. Pratt, and goes:

I stood once in a harbor as a ship was going out
On a voyage to a port beyond the sea...
And I heard the sailor promise to a lassie now in tears,
'When the fields are white with daisies I'll return.'

(Chorus) When the fields are white with daisies, and the

roses bloom again,
Let the love flame in your heart more brightly burn;
For I love you sweetheart only, so remember when
   you're lonely,
When the fields are white with daisies I'll return.

where have I been?/there and back again, to see how far it is. Fobbing-off phrase, but more likely between children than between an adult and a child – John Titford in an article from his column in *Family Tree Magazine* (December 1994). Partridge/*Catch Phrases* has 'there and back to see how far it is' as a child's response to 'where are you going?'

(I am going to) where the wicked cease from troubling and the weary are at rest. 'My dear old mother had this favourite saying on the subject of going to bed' – T. Braun, London SW3 (1997). This is a slight adaptation of Job 3:17: 'There the wicked cease from troubling; and there the weary be at rest' (referring to death). In Robert Louis Stevenson, *Treasure Island*, Chap. 7 (1883), Jim Hawkins revisits the 'Admiral Benbow' and notes: 'The captain, who had so long been a cause of so much discomfort, was gone where the wicked cease from troubling.'

where was Moses when the light went out? This 'almost proverbial' riddle (as the Opies call it in *The Lore and Language of Schoolchildren*, 1959) may have a precise answer:

Q. Where was Moses when the light went out?
A. In the dark.

The Opies found that in *The Riddler's Oracle* (1821). Miss

M.L. King, London SW3, said (1993) the answer 'according to my brother in the twenties was: "Running round the table with his shirt hanging out".'

The 1968 film *Where Were You When the Lights Went Out?* was inspired by the great New York blackout of 1965 when the electricity supply failed and, it was popularly believed, the birth-rate shot up nine months later. The phrase echoes our riddle and the lyrics of an American song: 'Where was Moses when the light went out? / Down in the cellar eating sauerkraut.' This is from the song 'Where Was Moses When the Light Went Out?' (1878) by John J. Stamford (?1840–99) and may, ultimately, allude to the plague of darkness in Egypt (Exodus 10:21–3).

...which was a lot of money in those days. One of Denis Norden's list of old person's phrases, recalled on BBC Radio *Quote...Unquote* (21 May 1996).

whimwam for a goose's bridle/for ducks to perch on/for a treacle mill/to wind the sun up. Fobbing-off phrases. 'In my childhood there was one particular saying my mother used, which I have never heard anywhere else. If she was making something and I became too inquisitive and asked what it was, it was always the same answer: "It's a wimwam for a duck's bridle." In other words, mind your own business' – Mrs E. James, Somerset (1995). 'When we came home from school and asked hungrily "What's for lunch?" our mother replied curtly, "Whimwams for ducks to peak on"' – Owen Wainwright, Guernsey (1996). Graham Aldred said (1998) that his mother would always use this same phrase when she couldn't be bothered to give a full explanation in answer to the question 'Mum, what's that?' or 'What's it for?' 'When I asked what something was, my mother would say: "They are wimwams for goose's bridles to run through"' – Mike Killen (1998). 'My mum always said (and said that her mum always said), "Wigwams, for ducks to pee upon" when asked, "What's for tea?", or "What are you doing?", or anything she couldn't be bothered to answer' – Steve McGuigan (2000). 'My mother used to say, "A wig-wam to wind the sun up" or "Layalls for meddlers"' – John Alexander, Cheshire (2000). Indeed, compare LAROVERS FOR MEDDLERS ... Apperson has 'A whim-wam from Yocketon. A whim-wham to wind the sun up. [Answers by old folk to inquisitive young people who interrupt them]' – from *Cheshire Proverbs* (1917).

whisperers at the table shall breakfast in the stable. Nannyism. Claire Mackenzie, Edinburgh (1999) found this in Edward Eager, *Half Magic* (1954).

whistle. See HAVE A WHISTLE ...

(it's) white and spiteful out there. 'On a frosty cold day' (Wickenden).

who will lift the dog's tail if not himself? Informal proverb. 'My Latvian friend responded to a mention of "self-praise is no recommendation" [a proverb known since 1612] by saying: "In my country we have a saying, 'Who will lift the dog's tail if not himself?'" She went on to say that this arose from wolf packs – the leader chose himself and raised his tail' – Rosemary C. Black, West Midlands (1996).

who's she – the cat's aunt? 'My mother had a dislike of the pronoun "she". As a child, if ever I referred to her as "she" in the course of conversation, she would immediately interject: "Who's she, the cat's aunt?"' – Barry Gayton, Norfolk (1996). From Stella Gibbons, *Cold Comfort Farm*, Chap. 6 (1932): '"She comes from up at the farm"... "Who's 'she'? The cat's mother?" snapped the shawl. "Speak properly to the young lady".'

whoops, Jemima! 'I am always intrigued by a phrase which I seem to have picked up for use when some unexpected mishap nearly arises. On such an occasion, one feels obliged to say, "Whoops, Jemima!" But who was Jemima in the first place?' – J.G. Hills, Hampshire (1994).

Ah, a good question. Since the 19th century, the name 'Jemima' has been applied to (1) any servant girl (2) a chamber-pot. I don't think we need to look too far to find a situation in which 'Whoops, Jemima!' might have been spoken.

whore. See HEAVENS, ELEVEN...

why are we here?/because we're not all there. A favourite expression of the father of Mrs Monica Nash, Nottinghamshire (1995).

why bother? – no one is going to stop a galloping horse to look at *you*! 'When we looked in the mirror or took trouble with make-up, my grandmother would make this remark' – Miss K.E. Bagley, Gloucestershire (1994). Casson/Grenfell has this, as well as, 'Don't think yourself so pretty. Even if a man on a galloping horse did carry you off one dark night, he would drop you at the first lighted lamp post.'

why is a mouse when it spins?/the higher, the fewer. I mentioned this nonsense riddle on Channel 4's *Countdown* programme in 1987 and was amazed at the response I had from viewers. Most people remembered it being told to them by teasing parents in the 1920s and 30s. John Mack, Surrey, suggested that it originated in repartee between Jasper Maskelyne and Oswald Williams in magic shows at the St George's Hall in Langham Place, London, in about 1930. If not originated, he says, it was certainly much used by them.

Mrs Jean E. French, Berkshire, suggested that it might not be nonsensical if you substituted the word 'when' for 'why' in posing the riddle. From this I wondered whether it had anything to do with 'Hickory, dickory, dock, the mouse ran up the clock, the clock struck one, the mouse fell down...'

A variation of the riddle (which doesn't help either) is: Q. Why is a mouse when it's spinning its web?/A. Because the more the fewer the quicker.

Other viewers raked up these equally nonsensical riddles: Q. How is a man when he's out?/A. The sooner he does, the much; Q. What is the difference between a duck?/A. One of its legs is both the same; Q. Which would you rather, or go fishing? [or swimming/hunting?] A. One rode a horse and the other rhododendron. This last may not be a riddle at all and the answer belong elsewhere.

Partridge/*Slang* gives 'What shall we do, or go fishing' as a 'trick elaboration' of the straightforward 'What shall we do now?' It is quoted in Dorothy L. Sayers, *The Nine Tailors*, (1934). Compare: 'Which would you rather be – or a wasp?'

why keep a cow when you can buy a bottle of milk? A common justification for not getting married. Hence, the comic confusion of this version: 'Why go out for a pint of milk when you've got an old cow at home?' Partridge/*Slang* also finds this 'cynical male gibe at marriage' in the forms 'Why buy a book when you can join a library?' and 'You don't have to buy a cow merely because you are fond of milk', dating them both from the late 19th century. He also suggests that the 'milk/cow' argument features in John Bunyan's *The Life and Death of Mr Badman* (1680), though this has not been verified and is probably not used in connection with marriage. Apperson also finds the simple expression 'Who would keep a cow when he may have a quart of milk for a penny?' by 1659.

widows. See GO AND SHED...

wife. See GO AND SHAKE HANDS...

wig. See DASH MY WIG!

wigs on the green. 'My wife's mother used to say over her shoulder as she left the house, "Don't let the cat get the tongs or wigs will be on the green"' – Peter Tatton-Brown, Devon (1998). Nothing to do with theatrical 'see you on the green', this one. It is apparently of Irish origin. In the days when people wore wigs, they were likely to end up on the grass if there was a fight. *OED2* has this from *Chambers Journal* (1 March 1856): 'If a quarrel is foreseen as a probable contingency, it is predicted that "there'll be wigs on the green".' *Wigs On the Green* became the title of a novel (1935) by Nancy Mitford.

(looking like the) wild woman of Borneo. Suzanne Hinton, East Sussex, had me floored when she wrote (2000): 'I was a child whose curly hair tended to be rather unruly. Whenever the wind turned the unruly to the frankly dishevelled, my mother would say to me, "Here's the Wild Woman of Borneo." Who was this amazing woman? Was she fact or fiction?' My first thought was that there must have been some fairground freak with this sobriquet – like 'The Boneless Wonder' so memorably evoked by Winston Churchill to describe Ramsay Macdonald on one occasion – but now I think not. Ian Forsyth, Co. Durham, suggested that the term is simply a variation on 'Wild Man of Borneo', the old name for the somewhat hairy and unkempt orang-outang. Indeed, the meaning of that animal's name, however you spell it, is either 'wild man' or 'man of the woods'.

Marjorie Wild, Devon commented (2001); 'This was one of my mother's oft-used expressions. It got me into trouble once when I was nursing at a nursing home in Croydon in the 60s. Going into the room of an elderly lady, to give her a "wash and brush up" in the early morning, I exclaimed, "Oh, Mrs —, you look like the wild woman of Borneo!" Soon after, I was summoned to the Matron, to whom Mrs — had complained. She'd spent years in India and felt I'd likened her to the natives. She'd have been even more upset if she'd known I was likening her to an orang-utang!'

W.A.R. Hamilton, Wiltshire (2000) recalled an Edwardian popular song along the lines of 'Old MacDonald had a farm'. The first verse consisted of the line 'The Wild Man of Borneo has just come to town' (repeated four times), the second verse, 'The wife of the Wild Man of Borneo...', the third verse, 'The son of the Wild Man of Borneo...', and so on through the family. Could this have encouraged use of this expression?

As to whether the 'wild *man* of Borneo' was ever invoked when referring to males. Eric Dunkley (2001) told me that when he was young and had a good head of hair, his mother used to tell him to comb it 'otherwise you'll look like the wild man from Borneo'. This masculine version also appears in the novel *Thin Ice* by Compton Mackenzie (1956).

Will. See IT'S DARK/BLACK...

willy. See WHAT A NICE NEW ONE...

Winchcombe. See DO YOU COME FROM...

wind. See LIKE THE BARBER'S CAT...

windows. See DON'T FEEL LIKE...

wing. See BIRD NEVER FLEW...

winter. See IT'S THE SIGN OF...

(well) wish in one hand and shit in the other and see which gets filled first. 'If you said "I wish..."' (Wickenden). Partridge/*Catch Phrases* points out that this saying may be alluded to in Swift's *Polite Conversation* (1738) – though possibly with 'piss/prick in the other' – when the Colonel is hastily interrupted saying, 'Wish in one Hand – '.

wishes. See IF WISHES WERE...

(don't) wonder till the rooks build a nest in your backside, then wonder how they got the sticks up there. 'When "I wonder" was said' (Wickenden).

(he) won't go out of sight of the smoke from his chimney. 'On my Dad never wanting to go away from home on holiday' (Wickenden).

wooden. See PUTTING A POULTICE...; RUNS IN THE FAMILY LIKE...; TOO LATE, TOO LATE...; UP THE WOODEN HILL/STAIRS...

woossit. See WHAT A WORLD...

words. See HOW MUCH DOES IT...

work. See NEVER SHOW A FOOL...

world. See WHAT A WORLD...

worms. See I'LL GO OUT INTO...

(it's the) worse the wear for being new so soon. 'My mother would say this, when I was a lad in the 1920s, talking about an article of clothing which was getting worn' – E.W. Wright, Suffolk (1995).

worse things happen at sea. This consolatory phrase was first recorded in 1829 (Pierce Egan, *Boxiana*) in the form 'Worse accidents occur at sea!' Casson/Grenfell has it as a nannyism. *Worse Things Happen at Sea* was the title of a play by Keith Winter, presented at London in April 1935. Compare what the mother of Marjorie Wild, Devon (2000), said to children who made a fuss over being hurt: 'That's nothing on a big ship.'

(it's) worse when there's none. 'When there was not much to be had of anything' (Wickenden).

worsted. See LIKE AN OLD WOMAN...; WHAT A WORLD...

(you look like) 'The Wreck of the Hesperus'. 'A family

saying that I did not resolve for almost fifty years was why, if I came in untidy or windswept, my mother always said, "You look like the Wreck of the Hesperus!"' – Janet M. Carr, Isle of Wight (1997). In fact, this used to be a common expression for 'in a mess, in a sad state'. The reference is to the title of Longfellow's poem (1839), much recited in Victorian days and relating the actual shipwreck of a schooner off the coast of New England. It contains such immortal lines as: 'The skipper he stood beside the helm,/His pipe was in his mouth.' The skipper has unfortunately taken his daughter along with him and when a hurricane blows up, he lashes her to the mast – and that's where she's found washed up the next morning.

Partridge/*Catch Phrases* dates the use of this to the late 19th century. 'The Wreck of the Hesperus' is also referred to in the song 'Lydia, the Tattooed Lady' (lyrics by E.Y. Harburg, music by Harold Arlen, 1939) as though it were commonly known as a picture.

wrestle. See NEVER WRESTLE WITH...

YZ

Y's a crooked letter. Fobbing-off phrase to children who ask 'why?' questions – Valerie Grosvenor Myer, Cambridgeshire (1996). 'Because Y is a crooked letter and can't be straightened' – Stella Richardson, Essex (1998). Another way of dealing with 'why?' is to reply 'Z' – Christopher Matthew on BBC Radio *Quote...Unquote* (13 October 1998).

yard. See FACE LIKE A YARD...

York. See RIDE TO...

you are a bigger liar than Tom Pepper. 'When I was younger, my mother used to say of certain people that they "told more lies than Tom Pepper". I have never found a reference for this insult' – Peter Dawson (1999). Partridge/*Slang* has a citation for this nautical name for a liar, dating from 1818. Tom Pepper was, apparently, 'the sailor who was kicked out of Hell for lying.' Apperson has from *Dialect of Leeds* (1862): 'A noted propagator of untruths is "as big a liar as Tom Pepper".'

you can always look down and pick nothing up. 'My

mother was very fond of saying this – it usually meant, "try to better yourself rather than take the easy option"' – R. Dixon, Staffordshire (1992). Partridge/*Slang* has this as 'You can always stoop and pick up nothing!' and considers it mostly of cockney use and a 'remark made by a friend after a "row" or by a parent concerning a child's intended husband (or wife).'

you can't expect a Duchess for sixpence. 'At school in England we used to get into trouble for airily saying this...' – Jon and Rumer Godden, *Two Under the Indian Sun* (1966). Presumably, this is the same as 'you can't make a silk purse out of a sow's ear'.

you could argue/talk the hind legs off a donkey. Nannyism (Casson/Grenfell) (which also has 'you'll eat the hind leg off a donkey'). D.S. Halley, Cheshire, rightly wondered (1996) why one says this to mean (a) talking with unflagging and wearying persistence, or (b) having the power to persuade another by eloquent or charming speech (to quote the *Oxford English Dictionary*'s definitions). Why indeed? And what does it really mean? Interestingly, the donkey is not important – in 1808 William Cobbett used the expression involving the hind leg of a horse. There is an Australian citation from 1879 incorporating the hind leg of a dog. There are also versions citing a bird's leg (understandably not hind-leg) and, from Lancashire, 'the leg off a brass pan'.

you could guess horse muck twice. 'One of my late mother's favourite sayings, when asked a question to which she thought the answer was fairly obvious, was, "You could guess 'oss-muck twice, and be right third time!" I don't know where it came from originally, but it is what she would have described as "a good old Yorkshire expression"' – A.J. Finn, East Yorkshire (1993).

you could ride bare-arsed to London on that. 'Referring to a blunt knife' (Wickenden). 'My old nanny – who rejoiced in the name of Mary Anne Hannaford Pulleyblank – when given a blunt knife to use, would say in a strong Devon accent: "You could ride to London on this and not tear your breeches"' – Mrs Diana Barber, Kent (1995). Casson/Grenfell has: 'These knives are so blunt you could ride to Romford on them', and this is obviously a development of Swift's *Polite Conversation* (1738) version: 'Well, one may ride to Rumford upon this Knife, it is so blunt.' Why Romford, one wonders? Compare RIDE TO YORK.

you have made your bed and now you must eat it. Nannyism. A play upon the proverb 'As you make your bed, so you must lie on it', which was known by the 16th century (according to the *CODP*).

you have to eat a peck of dirt before you die. 'When we were children and fussy with our food, my grandmother used to say: "Don't worry. You have to eat a peck of dirt before you die"' – Alison Vallins, East Sussex (1994). Grandmother was not alone. Casson/Grenfell has: 'You've got to eat a peck of dirt before you die' and Swift's *Polite Conversation* (1738) has: 'Poh, you must eat a Peck of Dirt before you dye.' This proverbial saying is quite widespread, though Apperson first finds it in 1639 in the form, 'You must eat a peck of ashes ere you die.' The actor Lee Simpson recalled on BBC Radio *Quote…Unquote* (16 May 1995) that his nanny from Norfolk preferred: 'You've got to shift a ton of muck before you die.'

you know what thought did – killed the cat and only thought he did it. 'When as children we said we "thought something", my Yorkshire Grandma would say: "You know what thought did – killed the cat and only thought he did it". My Edinburgh husband knows the expression as, "…planted a chicken thinking it would grow a hen"' – Margaret Barrow, Buckinghamshire (1995). Compare 'Do you know what thought did? It followed a donkey-cart and thought it was at a funeral' – said by the paternal grandmother of Kathleen B. Crossen, Belfast (1997). Or '…he followed a muck cart and thought it was a wedding' – Stella Richardson, Essex (1998). Partridge/*Slang* also lists these continuations: 'Ran away with another man's wife', 'Lay in bed and beshit himself, and thought he was up', and 'No, 'e never! 'E only thought 'e did!'

you might as well smoke here as hereafter. 'When my mother caught me smoking in my early teens, she said, "Well, you might as well smoke here as hereafter"' – Douglas S. Caldwell, Warwickshire (1996).

you must suffer in order to be beautiful. Nannyism (Casson/Grenfell). The origin of this statement has not been determined. It is usually regarded as a French saying: '*Il faut souffrir pour être belle*' – and that is how it is given as the title of a George Du Maurier cartoon in *Punch* (29 May 1880). The caption explains: 'The scene depicted above is not so tragic as one might suppose. It merely represents that best of husbands, Jones, helping the lovely Mrs J. to divest herself of her jersey.'

you talk like a ha'penny book without any leaves in it. 'I was told this, as a schoolgirl, if I dared to argue with my father' – Mrs Joyce Ball, Staffordshire (1998). Casson/

Grenfell has the nannyism: 'I can read you like a ha'penny book with the leaves out.'

you won't feel the benefit of it later. Nannyism (Casson/Grenfell). 'When someone called during the colder months of the year and seemed likely to stay for more than a few minutes, it was customary to say, "Won't you take off your coat? Or you won't feel the benefit of it when you go out"' – Brian Cooke, Gloucestershire (1993). Compare these words of wisdom from the family of Derek Robinson, the writer on what to say about clothing when the weather's bad: 'If you've got it, you can always put it on, but if you haven't got it, you can't take it off' – recalled on BBC Radio *Quote ... Unquote* (18 December 1990).

you'd be late for your own funeral. Nannyism.

you'd laugh to see your mother's nose on fire! 'If I was acting silly, laughing at nothing, this was what my mother would say. I thought this very unfair because I was sure I would not...' – Mrs P. Hogan, London N2 (1994).

you'll just have to wait until your hurry is over. 'On someone exclaiming they're in a hurry' (Wickenden).

you'll never get lost as long as you have got a tongue in your head. 'Although my mother could not read, she travelled all around Kent and she always said this' (Wickenden).

you're as daft as a penny watch/you're as hopeless as Percy Topliss! 'If I did anything silly, this is what my mother used to say' – Kathleen Smith, Moray (1994).

you're big enough and ugly enough. Parental put-down – father of Germaine Greer, as recalled in her book *Daddy, We Hardly Knew You* (1989).

you've been a bit early of late... 'I should like to share with you a saying of my late father's, which was sometime before the Second World War. He would often come out with, "You've been a bit early of late, you used to be behind before, but now you're first at last." No explanation was ever given for this, so I assume it was a compliment from one person to another on timekeeping' – Ray Parkerson, Hertfordshire (1993). Paul Beale commented: 'Compare "We're all square now, but we'll be round again shortly", which I heard from an army acquaintance, late 1950s.'

you've got to summer and winter a man before you can pretend to know him. An old country maxim, quoted in Flora Thompson, *Candleford Green* (1943). On BBC Radio *Quote...Unquote* (7 April 1992), Hunter Davies gave a version on the attitude of Cumbrian folk to newcomers in the Lake District: 'You winter them, you summer them, you winter them again, and then you say hello.'

your nose smells against rain. 'If you turned up your nose at some unpleasant odour' – mother of E.W. Wright, Suffolk (1995).

your nose will never go rusty. 'If one was being inquisitive' – Miss O.E. Burns, West Midlands (1995).

yum, yum, pig's bum! A commonly-known way of expressing that food is delicious. The actor Robin Bailey remembered it as a 'Black Country' saying, in the form

'Our mam, pig's bum' on BBC Radio *Quote...Unquote* (31 August 1985). Martin Baxter, West Yorkshire (1999), told me that he thought it was customarily completed with: '...apple sauce and chewing gum.' On *Quote...Unquote* (10 May 1994), the actress Helen Atkinson Wood coupled it with two other rhyming lines: 'Liar, liar, pants on fire' and 'Super dooper, Gary Cooper'. I myself have adopted 'Yum, yum, pig's bum!' and say it frequently...